MM AMERICAN **MARKETING** ASSOCIATION

The
Focus
Group
Research
Handbook

HOLLY EDMUNDS

NTC Business Books
NTC/Contemporary Publishing Group

Library of Congress Cataloging-in-Publication Data

Edmunds, Holly.
    The focus group research handbook / Holly Edmunds.
       p.   cm.
    Includes index.
    ISBN 0-8442-0288-6 (cloth)
    ISBN 0-658-00248-1 (paper)
    1. Focus group interviewing—Handbooks, manuals, etc.
I. American Marketing Association.   II. Title.
H61.28.E36   1999
001.4'33—dc21   98-33528
                                            CIP

Cover design by Jeanette Wojtyla
Interior design by Jeanette Wojtyla

Published by NTC Business Books in conjunction with the American Marketing Association
A division of NTC/Contemporary Publishing Group, Inc.
4255 West Touhy Avenue, Lincolnwood (Chicago), Illinois 60712-1975 U.S.A.
Copyright © 1999 by NTC/Contemporary Publishing Group, Inc.
Printed in the United States of America
International Standard Book Number: 0-8442-0288-6 (cloth)
                                     0-658-00248-1 (paper)
00 01 02 03 04 05 LB 19 18 17 16 15 14 13 12 11 10 9 8 7 6 5 4 3 2 1

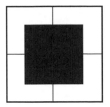

Contents

Chapter 5: Focus Group Evaluation 87

Chapter 6: Pros and Cons of Doing It Yourself 99

Chapter 7: Other Focus Group Situations 103

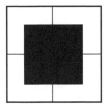

Introduction

This book is designed to cover the needs of two groups of readers. First, it is intended to serve as a handbook for the layperson who may need to contract with a professional marketing research vendor for a focus group study. For such readers, this book will explain the best uses of the methodology, the steps involved in the focus group research process, questions to ask the research vendor, and what to expect the vendor to deliver. It should also help in developing the objectives for a focus group study and provide a basic understanding of how to interpret and use the results of such a study. Although this handbook presents moderating techniques and discussion flows, they are not intended as a means of training the layperson to become an internal moderator for his or her company. A person wishing to achieve the necessary level of skill should instead enroll in a professional training program.

The second audience intended for this handbook is moderators and project managers with limited experience. For these readers, the book offers guidelines for designing and conducting focus group studies, including sampling and recruiting, discussion guide development, suggested moderating techniques, and reporting methods. It does not purport to provide the only answers in these areas, but rather it offers options to make the focus group process easier and more useful. In particular, it may help your clients (or you as a client) to better understand the different types of focus groups and their uses.

As is often the case with books covering such a detailed subject matter, readers might pick up the book to refer to a particular chapter, thereby missing important definitions in earlier chapters. To fill in the resulting gaps in information, a glossary of focus group–related terminology is provided at the end of the book. Terms included in the glossary are highlighted in *boldface italics* when they first appear in the text.

Focus Groups

" I have a great idea! What do you think about . . . ?" How many brainstorming sessions in the workplace begin like this? Yet having a great idea does not guarantee it will succeed with your customers. This is why companies often test their ideas using *focus group* research.

A focus group typically brings together eight to ten qualified people for a face-to-face discussion of a particular topic. (Groups of over ten participants tend to be somewhat unwieldy; interactions among the participants are less effective, and discussions can be hard to control.) Variations of this format— such as smaller groups and groups conducted on the telephone or over the Internet—meet specific needs and are described at the end of the chapter. This chapter also introduces general criteria for deciding when focus group research is appropriate, as well as the general content of a focus group study.

Use of Focus Groups

Exploring how customers will respond to a new idea is one example of when focus group research would be useful. Typically focus groups are used as a means of testing concepts, new products, and messages. A focus group is **qualitative research**, which means that you do not obtain results with percentages, statistical testing, or tables. Instead, this methodology is less structured than surveys or other **quantitative research** and tends to be more exploratory as well.

Rather than providing quantifiable responses to a specific question obtained from a large sampling of the population, focus group participants provide a flow of input and interaction related to the topic or group of topics that the group is centered around. While they appear to be less formal than a survey, focus groups do provide an important source of information for making business decisions. It is important, however, to ensure that persons using the results of such a qualitative study understand how to correctly interpret the resulting information.

Quantitative research provides results that can be generalized to a specific population, because it is based on a statistical sampling of the target population. The results of qualitative research, such as focus groups, however, are *not* quantifiable. They reflect only a very small segment of the **target market** in question. Given the number of focus group participants, results are not necessarily representative of the general population from which participants are recruited and should not be considered as such.

What focus groups offer instead is a more in-depth understanding of the target's perspectives or opinions than is otherwise obtainable through telephone interviews or mail surveys. Quantitative studies can miss subjective elements in, for example, a purchase maker's decision process. Focus groups, on the other hand, allow researchers to capture subjective comments and evaluate them. This methodology is exploratory, with its intent being to provide an understanding of perceptions, feelings, attitudes, and motivations.

When to Use and When to Avoid Focus Groups

Focus groups are best used when the concept or idea you wish to evaluate is new and when the best evaluation comes from letting the target customer (who can be either a consumer or a customer in the business-to-business sense) view the concept directly. A good example of this is a new advertising campaign. Typically, an advertising agency will want to test a new advertisement with the consumers it hopes to reach with the campaign. The agency needs to know whether the message is clear, whether consumers view the advertisement positively or negatively, whether the advertisement would prompt them to purchase the product, and so forth. The agency can explore these questions by showing the advertisement to consumers and discussing their reactions and their likes and dislikes. Their comments will allow the agency to fine-tune the advertisement or, if it is not well liked, to go back to the drawing board.

Another common use of focus group research is product concept testing. Participants in a group can discuss detailed diagrams and product descriptions, or they may test a product prototype in a hands-on fashion. This allows researchers to identify customer needs and attitudes regarding a concept before investing in further product development.

A focus group study also is often used to design the questionnaire for a quantitative survey. The focus group covers general issues on a topic, and respondents' comments often help researchers identify pertinent issues that might otherwise be left out of a survey. Hypotheses generated by focus groups frequently lead to further testing using quantitative methods. Alternatively, focus groups can be used to further interpret quantitative research. For example, if a telephone survey produces a significant percentage of unexpected comments on a certain topic, a focus group study could investigate the issue with greater depth.

Another particularly useful application of focus group research is as a brainstorming mechanism. If you have a problem to solve, this type of methodology often provides fresh insights regarding the issue at hand. It can also provide an excellent forum for generating creative ideas or new-product ideas for new markets, as well as generating new ideas for your established markets.

These, as well as some other potential uses of focus groups, are listed in Table 1-1.

In many other cases, conducting focus groups would *not* be advisable. Focus groups would not be an appropriate methodology, for example, in testing consumer reactions to a product for which there was no budget to change it if it tested negatively. A software package that is ready for release in three weeks is not a good candidate for a focus group study if the developer is not

Table 1-1 When to Use Focus Groups

To test new concepts

To evaluate advertising/copy

To evaluate promotions

To develop questionnaires

To generate ideas or support brainstorming

To position a product/service

To assess product usability

---

willing to make pertinent changes to the product based on comments from the groups. On the other hand, a group might prove useful for such a product in terms of messaging; that is, determining the product's strengths and weaknesses so the developer can emphasize its strengths in the marketing effort.

In addition, focus group research is not recommended if the end users of the focus group results are not completely comfortable with and aware of the types of results obtainable from the groups. Many years ago, when I was still on the vendor side of the business, I had a client who insisted on conducting focus groups to test his product among potential users. He was a marketing director and was one of my first clients as a consultant. I assumed that he was familiar with qualitative research and the results such studies produced. In addition, focus groups were the preferred methodology for the type of testing he had requested.

The groups went well, and we obtained a great deal of

valuable feedback. Furthermore, the focus groups yielded some excellent quotations for use in developing the firm's marketing strategy. When the report was completed, I met with my client, who was, to my surprise, extremely confused because I had neglected to include any tables or graphs of the data in my report. He could not be convinced that the recommendations were valid without solid numbers and percentages to back up the focus group results.

Unfortunately, this is not an unusual case. As noted earlier, focus group results are not representative or quantifiable. You simply cannot answer questions such as "How many . . . ?" or "How much . . . ?" with a qualitative research methodology. Therefore, you and your audience must be comfortable with qualitative analysis in order for the focus group results to be useful.

Another potential disadvantage of focus groups is that they may not be the best solution for studying extremely sensitive or personal issues such as certain medical conditions, politics, sex, or morals. A good rule of thumb is to ask yourself whether you would be open to discussing the topic in a room full of strangers (regardless of the amount you might be paid!).

Finally, focus groups should never be utilized to make a final decision. Consider focus groups only to be a "thermometer" that allows you to test the "temperature" of consumers' reactions to your research topic. As previously stated, this methodology is exploratory, so it is not statistically valid. It is only appropriate for investigative, fine-tuning, or concept-testing purposes. As such, it should be considered as only one aspect of the decision-making process, rather than as the process itself.

For a summary of when to avoid using focus groups, see Table 1-2.

Table 1-2 When Not to Use Focus Groups

To make a final decision

To explore extremely sensitive or personal topics

To answer "How many?" or "How much?"

To conduct research for an audience that doesn't understand the purpose of qualitative research

To evaluate a product, advertisement, etc., to which revisions will not be made despite the results of the study

To save the money or time required for quantitative research

To set prices for a product or service

Advantages and Disadvantages of Focus Groups

Provided that you have established that focus groups are the appropriate methodology for meeting your objectives, you should also recognize the advantages and disadvantages inherent in preparing for a focus group study. On a positive note, focus groups can be coordinated, conducted, and analyzed within a relatively short time period. *Probing* and *clarification* of participants' comments are easy to do in the focus group environment.

On the negative side, however, *recruiting* focus groups can be difficult, depending on the definition of qualified participants. In addition, participants' responses are not independent; they are generally offered in the context of a group's conversation. As a result, participants may respond differently regarding a specific issue than if they had been discussing the same topic, for example, during a telephone or *one-on-one interview*. Focus group studies, as viewed by a layperson, appear deceptively simple to design and coordinate: "Hey, what is there to it, really? I just need to get a few people in a room and let them discuss my product idea!" In reality, they are even more complex than most quantitative surveys. Not only must you identify and contact your research target, but you must convince them to, in most cases, drive to an unfamiliar site to share their opinions with a group of total strangers. This can appear somewhat daunting to anyone involved in the process.

General Design of a Focus Group Study

Let's begin with a general overview of the focus group process. Your focus group study begins with setting your *research objectives*. What specifically do you want to learn from the research you plan to conduct? Will your objectives be best met through a qualitative research methodology (as defined earlier in this chapter)? Your objectives should be centered around a common theme. You should not, for example, attempt to test a new PC and a new software product together in the same focus groups. It would become very difficult to distinguish which product was triggering which reactions. This is, of course, an extreme example, but it does show the importance of clear-cut objectives.

Once you have defined your objectives, you should identify a *recruiting profile*. Whom should you speak with? Who will best be able to answer your questions? The number of groups you conduct and the definition of your targets for the study depend on how many distinct markets you have and the general scope of your markets. If, for example, you are talking to consumers who own microwave ovens in the regions where you hope to test-market a new microwave food product concept, you should conduct at least two groups in each of the major markets in your regions. Then you should consider who does the shopping for these products. Are men doing more of the grocery shopping? (Check *secondary information* if it is available to confirm this!) If so, perhaps you should consider four groups in each city: two groups with men and two groups with women. If this exceeds the research budget, you could consider one focus group with men and one with women in each of the markets. Or has one region already proved less receptive to your microwave food line? Perhaps focus groups in that region would be a waste of resources, since it is unlikely you will heavily promote the product in that region anyway. These are the types of questions you need to ask when determining which groups will provide the most valuable information and where they should be held.

Research using a single focus group is rare. It is advisable to conduct two or more groups, frequently in several markets, depending on the breadth of the topic. This ensures the best representation of the target market and allows comparisons between different groups. Although the budget is understandably a concern in any company, it is important to ensure that marketing research is done correctly to yield the most reliable results. If you try to save money by cutting back on, for example, the number of groups conducted, you may miss important information from a region, a segment, and so on.

You must also select a site (typically a marketing research facility) in each city where the groups will be conducted. Generally, the same research firm that handles the recruiting for the study will also provide the focus group facility for a set fee. A major factor in selecting a focus group location is accessibility to potential participants.

Recruiting is most frequently conducted by telephone, with interviewers screening contacts via a series of brief questions to determine whether or not they qualify to participate in the study based on your preestablished recruiting profile. The *screener questionnaire* may well be the most important tool used in the focus group research. This brief questionnaire asks a series of questions to evaluate whether a contact is eligible to discuss the topic at hand. If, for example, you are testing a new software program, it would not make sense to conduct the discussion with persons who never use a personal computer.

Once they have been qualified, potential participants are invited to attend the group. Typically, they are offered a *"co-op," or cooperation, fee* (generally in the form of cash) to capture their interest as well as to help compensate for any peripheral costs involved in attending the group (for example, mileage, parking, time). The amount depends on whom you are speaking with, what the topic is, what the expected length of the group is, and how far the participants must commute. High-level managers or professionals typically receive between $100 and $200, while generally consumers may receive between $35 and $75. A relatively high amount should be offered when the discussion subject matter is complex. The amount also depends on the city in which the groups are being conducted (fees are higher, for example, in New York City than in Topeka, Kansas).

Dependent on the focus group client as well as the participants, co-op payments other than cash may be offered. For instance, a restaurant chain conducting focus groups might offer gift certificates. Firms conducting focus groups with doctors or other highly paid professionals might offer participants the choice of cash or a donation to their favorite charitable organization. Promotional incentives such as mugs and T-shirts may also be offered, but only in certain cases and with appropriate participants. For example, nonprofit organizations may not have the budget necessary to pay cash to participants but may have promotional items in stock. In such cases, it would be acceptable to use these items in lieu of cash co-op payments. With marketing-savvy consumers as today's norm, however, these nonmonetary forms of compensation are less likely to prove as successful as a cash payment.

As will be discussed in greater detail in the next chapter, recruiters typically overrecruit participants for each focus group session. This allows for several no-shows or last-minute cancellations without reducing the required number of focus group participants. If too many recruits show up for a given focus group session, it is customary to pay the full co-op amount promised to all of them, even if some are released to return home.

It is not unusual for some participants to arrive after the focus group has started. The moderator will generally allow late arrivals to join the group up to five or even ten minutes late, particularly if the group is smaller than anticipated. If someone is later than the preestablished cutoff time, he or she is usually released from attending the group to avoid any unnecessary disruption of the discussion already in progress. While you can technically refuse to provide co-op payments to these participants if they are released, it is generally considered a goodwill gesture to pay them regardless. A possible exception to this rule would be if someone arrives an hour late without a reasonable excuse!

While recruiting is under way, typically the client and/or vendor will be developing the *discussion guide* for the groups. This is a general outline of the issues to cover during the discussion, including specific questions to be asked as well as potential probes the *moderator* might use to stimulate additional discussion in a given area. The moderator will follow this outline during the groups, although the conversation may flow in a different order than initially outlined. The moderator's main purpose is to keep participants on track and to ensure that all participants are given an opportunity to present their views and suggestions during the 90 to 120 minutes required for a focus group discussion.

Focus groups are typically videotaped as well as audiotaped to better enable whoever is writing the focus group report to refer to specific questions and review crucial aspects of the discussion. Reporting, as mentioned earlier, varies significantly from quantitative reports in that there are no graphs or percentages. Rather, the report groups comments indicating general attitudes leaning in one direction or another, and it often includes direct quotations from participants. Conclusions are based primarily on the majority of the responses, although it is not uncommon to note unexpected comments that arise during the discussions in order to allow consideration of all possible sides of a given issue.

Variations on Focus Groups

As indicated at the beginning of this chapter, there are a number of variations on what is typically considered a standard focus group format (eight to ten participants in a conference room setting, viewed by clients seated behind a one-way mirror). These various group formats include the following:

- Telefocus groups

- Mini groups

- Triads (or dyads)

- Internet focus groups

- Video focus groups

The decision whether to use standard focus groups or one of these variations should be based on the research objectives. For example, as a general rule of thumb, studies covering extremely technical or emotional subjects are more successful when fewer participants are involved in the focus group discussion.

Compared to the standard format, these variations are likely to result in significant cost savings. But bear in mind that the objectives of your study should take precedence when selecting a group size and type. Do not settle on moderating groups via telephone if your objectives dictate that your concept requires face-to-face explanations. Likewise, do not opt for smaller groups to save money when you are likely to get more detailed information on reactions to an advertising campaign from a standard-sized group.

The remainder of this chapter provides more details about the nonstandard focus group formats, including the usage, benefits, and disadvantages of each.

Telefocus Groups

Basically, *telefocus groups* are just what they sound like: focus groups conducted via telephone. Recruiting is conducted by telephone in the same manner as for standard focus groups. On the days of the scheduled groups, however, focus group participants dial into a toll-free teleconferencing number approximately ten minutes prior to their scheduled group time and provide the operator with their predesignated password in order to gain access to the group. At the start of the group, they are connected with the moderator and all of the other group participants. Likewise, the research sponsor(s) can call into a designated number and be put into a listening mode, where they are able to listen to the group discussion without being heard themselves. When using this format, it is preferable to aim for slightly smaller groups (six or seven participants), in order to allow the moderator to maintain better control over the group.

Clients can also send messages to the moderator via an operator on the conference line. The client signals the operator, for example, by dialing a prespecified code. The operator then comes on the client's line, takes the message, and relays it to the focus group moderator. The process is surprisingly similar to that utilized in a standard focus group situation.

The moderator conducts the telefocus groups in a manner very similar to an in-person group. The group participants are instructed to state their name prior to each time they offer their comments so that they can be readily recognized by the moderator, all other participants, and those listening to the groups (and later to the audiotapes). Group sessions are audiotaped for the purposes of documentation and analysis. Co-op payments or other predetermined incentives are mailed to participants following the groups.

Advantages of Telefocus Groups

Telefocus groups are beneficial in several different ways:

- They cut the costs associated with the traditional focus group research project.

- They speed up the research process.

- Using the phone allows groups to be conducted even when geographically standard groups would not be feasible.

- Telefocus groups offer a methodology that avoids bringing together participants who could be competitors.

- The format increases convenience and comfort levels for participants, which in turn simplifies the recruiting process.

Using a telefocus group versus an in-person group can potentially reduce costs by as much as one-third. Although there are still design costs, recruiting, moderating, reporting, and co-op fees, other costs are reduced or eliminated. These include the client and moderator's travel expenses, facility rentals, refreshments, hostessing, and videotaping.

Telefocus groups also provide a *fast* alternative to standard focus groups. Cutting out the travel associated with the usual focus group process allows groups to be completed more rapidly. This means the results of the study will be available sooner.

Occasionally, it may be necessary to conduct focus groups using a sample that is large in scope but without adequate contacts in any single region. The telefocus group methodology allows each group to consist of participants from various cities, states, or regions. Likewise, if there are no proven differences among regions regarding a given service or product, the research team can conduct national groups.

This particular focus group variation also provides a viable solution when competitors are being recruited to participate in the same focus group. For example, if computer resellers were to attend a focus group in their own city, a participant could easily be sitting at the table with a major competitor from down the block. This can greatly limit the amount (and quality) of information you can obtain from the focus group. Using a telefocus group, you can recruit from a wider area, thus reducing the competitive threat that would have made participants reluctant to participate openly.

Telefocus groups tend to be much more convenient for the participants. Participants do not have to drive to a facility, locate parking, and so forth. Rather they can dial into the groups from home, the office, or wherever it is most convenient for them. Furthermore, they are not faced with the sometimes unnerving prospect of sitting around the table with total strangers. Speaking on the phone appears to reduce "stage fright"; participants seem to be less intimidated by those who are more talkative. Given the increased convenience and comfort level for participants, it can be easier to recruit participants for this type of focus group.

In addition, telefocus groups may prove useful for dealing with relatively sensitive topics. Participants can speak freely without seeing or being seen by their fellow participants.

Disadvantages of Telefocus Groups

As with any research methodology, consideration of conducting telefocus groups should weigh the possible disadvantages:

- The effectiveness of focus group topics/discussion may be limited by the format.

- Stronger moderator skills are necessary.

- Visual cues from participants' reactions and body language are lost.

- Group dynamics are limited compared to those achievable in standard focus groups.

- Crossing geographical lines may generate slightly different results.

Telefocus groups have distinct limitations in terms of what objectives they can meet. They are not effective, for example, in instances where participants need to test a product, view a concept, or listen to any lengthy explanation. Highly technical discussions are also extremely difficult via telefocus groups because it is easy for the moderator to lose the group's attention by using jargon or highly technical terminology throughout the groups.

This focus group format also requires that the moderator have extremely strong skills. He or she is put in the somewhat unusual position of not being able to see the group participants. This situation makes it more difficult to identify quieter respondents, who should be encouraged to speak up. In addition, the telefocus group moderator must work harder to maintain the group participants' attention.

The moderator is not the only one facing challenges related to loss of visual cues in a telefocus group situation. The clients who are listening to the groups lose the added benefit of the participants' reactions to comments others make. Body language, which can also measure participants' attitudes, is lacking in this process altogether.

Telephone interactions between participants and with the moderator differ greatly from those in in-person groups. It is not always immediately clear to participants that someone has spoken directly to them, because they can't see the participant addressing them or were not identified by name. Conversations are also punctuated by participants giving their names before each comment, which tends to slow the flow of the discussion.

On any given focus group topic, there remains the potential for regional reactions to a concept. Telefocus groups, which can cross geographical lines, run the risk of blurring these differentiations. The phone groups can, however, be recruited to be conducted in specific markets, just as would be done with standard groups.

Mini Focus Groups

A *mini focus group* differs only slightly from a standard focus group. Rather than including eight to ten participants in a group, this methodology typically includes five or six participants. These groups are conducted as standard groups are, in a conference room setting with a moderator and videotaping.

Mini groups still tend to require between ninety minutes and two hours in order to adequately cover the discussion topics. And, as with the other methodologies discussed, overrecruiting is recommended; generally eight or nine qualified contacts should be recruited to guarantee a group size of five or six participants.

Conducting smaller groups offers some benefits:

- With fewer participants, there is more emphasis on the topic and less on polling the participants.

- Mini groups allow greater observational opportunities— more chances to do hands-on testing than is possible in larger groups.

- With fewer participants, there are lower recruiting costs and co-op fees.

These benefits are similar to those that will be detailed for triads and dyads.

Triads

As their name suggests, *triads* consist of three participants, making them smaller than standard or mini focus groups. They are conducted in a focus group setting, typically with clients viewing the groups from behind the one-way mirror. Groups are conducted by a moderator and videotaped as in the standard group format. (Occasionally research firms conduct **dyads**, or discussions with two participants.)

Because more ground can be covered with only three participants, however, the triad groups tend to be briefer than standard or mini groups. They usually require from one hour to one hour and fifteen minutes, rather than the usual hour and a half to two hours typically required for larger group discussions. As with standard in-person focus groups, it is a general practice to overrecruit for triads. Recruiting five or six potential participants allows for no-shows and last-minute cancellations.

Advantages of Triads

There can be benefits to utilizing triads:

- Triads allow greater detail with more in-depth probing on topics of discussion.

- They permit enhanced testing of new products, procedures, and so on.

- The format cuts some costs generally associated with larger groups.

These benefits are similar to those related to mini groups. Given the even smaller group size, however, the benefits are magnified.

With only three participants, it is easier to probe deeper on comments. The moderator can obtain more input and details from participants.

Triads allow better testing opportunities. It is easier, for example, to test a new software program with only three people in the group setting. There is more time to work with the group and discuss their opinions of the product than with a group of eight participants, where a large portion of the group time would have to be devoted to answering questions and getting them set up on the program.

Smaller groups offer better opportunities to observe participants' interactions with products. There is also a greater amount of control over product tests, as there are fewer chances for participants to watch how someone else does a task and then copy it themselves.

Furthermore, with triads there is less opportunity for groupthink. For instance, if participants are testing a new package feature, each participant can be brought individually into the room and allowed to offer opinions prior to a group discussion. With fewer people involved, time is more likely to be available to do this. Thus, you can obtain fresh viewpoints and immediate reactions from each participant, without bias from other participants.

With fewer participants, there are fewer incentives to pay, which can lower the overall project cost. (This, of course, is only the case if the study does not call for large numbers of triads.) As triads tend to be shorter in length, more groups can be conducted in one day/evening at a facility. This, in turn, can cut facility rental costs, as well as related hotel and meal expenses for the moderator and clients alike.

Disadvantages of Triads

There are, however, a number of disadvantages associated with this methodology:

- The triad format requires conducting more groups to obtain enough information for analysis.

- The format limits the variety of opinions offered; fewer opinions are available unless more groups are conducted.

- Triads require a strong moderator to minimize participants' discomfort.

With only three participants in a given group, the study will require more groups in order to cover the topic adequately and reach some general conclusions. You cannot rely on only two or three triads to provide solid input into the business decision process. Instead, as a rule of thumb, assume that you should conduct at least enough triads with each targeted segment to equal one standard focus group (three triads per segment).

While triads do provide some level of group discussion, the *variety* of opinions offered is obviously limited by the small group size. The trade-off is the depth of information obtained from the participants.

Triads can be more uncomfortable for participants because they are expected to participate more heavily than in larger, standard-sized groups. Triad participants have to speak up more often and answer questions in greater detail. A strong moderator is needed to minimize the discomfort that this environment can cause some participants.

Internet Focus Groups

As with telefocus groups, *Internet focus groups* are basically self-defining. This new focus group option has emerged with the rapidly increasing population of on-line users. These "virtual" focus group discussions create another set of benefits as well as different disadvantages.

Advantages of Internet Focus Groups

From a positive standpoint, focus groups conducted via the Internet offer several benefits that may make them attractive to clients:

- Using them speeds up the research process.

- They provide an effective channel for conducting research with on-line users.

- They cut costs associated with the traditional focus group research project.

- The anonymity of participants potentially leads to increased openness during the discussions.

- These groups can reach a broad geographic scope.

- They have potential to increase access to hard-to-reach participants, such as professionals and travelers.

- Participation is convenient and comfortable.

Internet focus groups provide a faster means of conducting focus groups than standard methodologies—potentially even faster than the use of the telefocus group methodology. This is because with this methodology, focus group participants are typically "prerecruited." Interested potential participants have already signed up with the on-line research vendor and completed their profile forms. Focus groups are recruited from this preestablished user base. This preestablished sample can increase the incidence of eligible respondents, thereby speeding up the recruiting process and reducing the time required to complete the entire focus group research project.

This particular methodology also provides an excellent made-to-order source of Internet users. These users, by virtue of completing their research profiles, have been prescreened, in effect, in terms of Internet usage.

Utilizing Internet focus groups inherently reduces certain costs. Specific costs that may be cut include sampling, recruiting, and expenses related to travel and the focus group facility (including room rentals, refreshments, hostessing, and taping).

Internet focus groups provide a high degree of anonymity. Participants can be identified in groups by their on-line service screen names. This degree of anonymity may enhance honesty and openness during focus group sessions. Participants are not likely to feel self-conscious, as they are not recognizable.

As with telefocus groups, Internet groups allow focus groups to consist of participants from a wide variety of cities, states, or regions. In fact, given the very nature of the Internet, this type of group is particularly flexible in terms of geographic scope, as usage is widespread worldwide.

Internet groups have the potential to increase access to hard-to-reach participants. For instance, the incidence in recruiting highly trained professionals such as doctors and lawyers is relatively low. Other people who are difficult to reach include frequent business travelers. These types of people are unlikely to be readily available to talk when a recruiter attempts to reach them by telephone. With Internet focus group recruiting, these people are prequalified and more likely to be easily reached via E-mail.

In addition to the comfort provided by the participants' anonymity with Internet focus groups, this methodology provides other convenience- and comfort-related benefits. As with telefocus groups, participants are spared the trip to a focus group facility. With Internet groups, they can participate from the location of their choice, given the necessary Internet access capabilities.

Disadvantages of Internet Focus Groups

Despite the positive aspects associated with Internet focus group research, there remain a number of negative issues to consider as well. These include the following concerns (similar to those related to telefocus groups):

- Focus group topics/discussions are limited.

- Visual cues are absent.

- Group dynamics are limited in comparison to standard focus groups.

- Crossing geographic boundaries may skew results slightly.

- The sample is limited to those already on the Internet and predisposed to participating.

- The client's confidentiality may be at a greater degree of risk.

To the extent that responses to Internet focus groups must be typed, highly technical topics may be difficult to conduct in a timely manner. Also, you are limited to the extent that you can test advertising, products, and concepts via this methodology.

With in-person focus groups, clients viewing the groups can see physical reactions to issues brought up during the discussion. With Internet focus groups, as with telefocus groups, this capability is lost.

Again, because of the typing and message time lapses involved in Internet focus groups, there may be fewer spontaneous comments and less "play" on a topic being discussed. As a result, groups may provide less depth of discussion than in other forms of focus groups. Participants potentially have more time to consider how to respond than in oral discussions, which are free of the forced lapse that occurs with the typing of responses.

The use of Internet groups suggests another issue: the possibility that crossing geographic boundaries may skew results slightly. For instance, in-person focus groups conducted on the East Coast, in the Midwest, and on the West Coast potentially will get regional responses to, say, an advertising concept. With Internet groups, these differences may not be apparent, as participants in a group can be national. (You could, however, alleviate this problem by targeting specific regions as with telefocus groups.)

The sample is limited to those predisposed to participating. Typically, participants for Internet focus groups indicate their willingness to participate in groups by signing up with the research company via the Internet. They provide a self-profile and then are contacted when there appears to be a fit for screening purposes. Unless you are specifically looking for Internet users, you may be disregarding a portion of your market by conducting groups in this manner. You also may be limiting your sample to "professional" focus group participants—those predisposed to joining a discussion group and/or who are interested in the cash potential of participation.

Finally, the client's confidentiality may be at a greater degree of risk. With Internet groups, it is even more difficult to ensure that you are not including competitors in a group. Likewise, if precautions are not taken, any materials participants view via the World Wide Web, even on secured sites, could be potentially printed and viewed outside of the context of the group.

Video Focus Groups

Videoconferencing has emerged as a popular alternative for companies focusing on reducing the skyrocketing costs of travel expenses as well as reducing employees' time away from the office. *Video focus groups* are actually standard focus groups conducted in person by a moderator. Clients view the groups via videoconference from another location (or several locations). Likewise, debriefings can be conducted long-distance with the moderator.

This is not, however, so much a new methodology in focus group research as it is a technological tool to allow cost cutting. Also, you are limited by the research vendor's capability to arrange such groups. If the vendor's facility is not equipped with the necessary equipment for videoconferencing, then the cost savings from not traveling could be eaten up by making these arrangements. If you consider utilizing the video focus group methodology, you should contact vendors who currently are set up to conduct these types of groups from their own sites. Finally, be prepared for potential technical difficulties and occasional lapses between when a comment is made and when you view the person speaking.

Designing a Focus Group Study

The design of a focus group study encompasses a number of tasks, all of which are crucial to the success of the study. In preparing for your study, you need to identify a *sample* source (the list of names you will recruit from), design the screener questionnaire, and develop the discussion guide. This chapter will provide instructions on how to accomplish these tasks in a way that will ensure that your study meets your project objectives.

Sampling for Focus Groups

It is important to consider what sample source you will use in recruiting your focus groups. Depending on your target and your research objectives, you might use customer lists. You might purchase (or have your research vendor purchase) lists from outside sources such as Dun & Bradstreet or other list brokers. Focus groups can also be recruited through random calling.

Whatever your sample source, however, it is very important to consider its potential accuracy. Many financial institutions, for example, utilize customer information files. These computerized systems can sort customers based on a wide variety of criteria, including age, zip code, deposit balances, and income. Income sources might not be readily available to the institution, so these figures could be appended to the system from outside database sources. In these cases, the income figures could be far from accurate and quite difficult to keep updated on a regular basis. If the bank were recruiting focus groups specifically targeting customers with income levels over $50,000, it would be advisable to ask a screening question to confirm income ranges, rather than to simply assume that the sample it was using was accurate.

Another issue that should be considered is the use of a facility's recruiting databases. Many recruiting firms have established databases with detailed profiles of past participants or, in some cases, persons indicating an interest in participating in future focus groups. Although these resources are frequently used to recruit focus groups, this practice is inappropriate, as it can encourage "professional participants" who are somewhat practiced in their responses and are more interested in the money than the process. Despite their limitations, these databases can prove helpful in some instances, particularly in cases where your target consists of hard-to-reach professionals such as physicians.

Design of the Screener Questionnaire

As noted in Chapter 1, the screener questionnaire may be the most important tool used in focus group research. The use of this pre–focus group survey enables you to correctly identify eligible participants for the focus group discussion. Screener questionnaires generally consist of between five and ten basic questions designed to determine whether contacts are qualified to attend the groups: In other words, are the contacts representative of the target market you need to investigate?

The screening process usually requires a brief time on the phone with each contact person, sometimes as little as five minutes. The screener is designed to appear as a mini survey. The *recruiter* invites qualified contacts to attend a group and leaves unqualified contacts feeling that they have completed a research study, unaware that they are not actually participating in the study itself.

The client should monitor a few initial recruitment interviews to ensure that the screener flows smoothly and that contacts are clear on what is being asked. Often recruitment firms have the capability to allow remote monitoring of the recruiting process. In these situations, clients can monitor the telephone screening interviews from off-site locations such as their own offices or homes.

Typical Questions

Screener questionnaires typically include questions that identify whether or not a contact person fits the group's proposed profile. These questions are based on the focus group topic and can include product purchase habits, car ownership, job title or responsibilities, decision-making authority, and so on, depending on the objectives of your study. Frequently, demographic questions such as age, income, and gender are also required.

For example, if you are conducting a series of focus groups regarding children's use of the Internet, you might be looking at several targets from which you would like to obtain input. These could be like the following breakdown:

- Young children between the ages of ten and thirteen

- Teens between the ages of fourteen and eighteen

and, for parental feedback:

- Parents of children in these prespecified age groups.

To qualify, contacts would not only have to fit into these categories, but also meet the following criteria:

- Have access (or have children who have access) to a personal computer at home or school

- Have regular access to one or more on-line services

- Use the Internet at least two hours per week

The questionnaire might include other questions, less for screening purposes than to obtain some additional information about *qualified* participants. For instance, responses might indicate how many have taken computer classes or training workshops, and what Web browser they primarily use.

These added questions might simply provide further information about participants without being set up as requirements to determine group participation. If, however, you determine that you want X participants in each group to have taken a computer class within the past year, then you would establish a *quota group*. Such a group defines how many recruits meeting the preestablished criteria are to be recruited for each focus group.

Quota groups can add greater depth to your discussions, but if too many are set, they may also make reporting more difficult by blurring results within each session. Quotas also increase the costs of recruiting by further limiting who is invited to participate in the research study. Choose quotas carefully. Which ones could provide valuable differentiations, and which ones are not necessary at this point in the research?

More frequently now, recruiters also ask potential focus group participants questions intended to help identify qualified persons who might be more comfortable speaking in a group discussion and/or appear most familiar with the topic to be discussed. These often consist of one or two open-ended questions, which are designed to allow contacts to respond in greater detail. The recruiters then rate the contacts regarding their attitudes, willingness to talk, familiarity with the subject matter, and so on. While the logic behind such questions is apparent, recruiters are not necessarily the best judges of how the dynamics of the focus group will work. A good moderator, rather than recruiters' opinions, is the real key to a fruitful focus group session.

Let's look at another example: screening questions for a focus group to test a series of new fast-food advertisements. For advertisements that are targeted at adults, it might be assumed that the most desirable participants for the focus groups would be men and women between the ages of eighteen and forty-five who purchase any type or brand of fast food. This assumption is based, for the purposes of this example, on the premise that college students and busy parents (both in this age range) are likely targets for the fast-food market. To qualify for this group, contacts would have to fit the preceding general profile and meet criteria such as these:

- Watch television and/or listen to radio programming at least ten hours per week

- Purchase (any) fast food one or more times per week for their own personal consumption

- Make their purchase decision based on preferred taste rather than price

Other potential screening questions might include whether they typically carry out or dine in at fast-food outlets and whether they ever purchase fast food for others (such as children or friends).

Invitation to Participate

While the screener questionnaire is designed to make contacts believe that they are participating in a telephone survey, once a contact is determined to be qualified for the research study, he or she must be invited to attend the groups. If the recruit is willing to attend, the recruiter provides additional information regarding the facility location and obtains mailing information in order to send out a *confirmation letter*.

The recruiter should request that participants arrive fifteen to twenty minutes prior to the scheduled group start time. This allows the participants to get somewhat comfortable with each other and to enjoy the refreshments provided. In addition, it discourages late arrivals from disrupting the group once it has started. Finally, it provides time for participants to complete any questionnaires or information forms required before the discussion.

Focus group recruits may ask whether they may bring their spouse or even friends along to the facility. This is particularly common when conducting focus groups with senior citizens, who may require a driver or simply be nervous about going to a group where they are unfamiliar with the people. Provided that the research facility has adequate "waiting room" space, it can be allowed. The recruiter should, however, make it very clear that the additional person(s) may *wait* for them but will not be allowed to join the actual focus group (even if the group is short one or more participants). Nor will these "visitors" be compensated for coming to the facility, as attendance is tracked! Typically, other than the courtesy of a cup of coffee, these additional people are also not provided with refreshments, which are ordered based on the number of participants (and not the participants' guests).

Similarly, focus group recruits occasionally ask whether they may bring their child(ren) along to the group. Interviewers should be sensitive to the fact that this might be the only way that certain recruits can actually be able to attend the sessions. Still, participants should not be allowed to bring children under eighteen years of age with them to the focus group facility. Facility owners would then be assuming liability for the children while the parent was participating in the group discussion. It is preferable to recruit a different participant than to deal with the additional difficulties that could arise in such circumstances.

Sample Questionnaire

Five examples of typical focus group screener questionnaires appear in Appendix A. These examples illustrate the important items to include in a screener questionnaire:

- *Identification of the research vendor*—This helps to legitimize the study by reassuring contacts that an actual research company is conducting the study. In cases where contacts are unsure of the study's legitimacy, they can be given a manager's name and number to call back and validate that the research company does exist. If the focus group study is not a **blind study**, then using the client's name in the screener may also help to legitimize the study.

- *General purpose of the study*—This sets the tone and expectations for the study. It gives a brief explanation of what participants can expect to talk about during the focus group discussion. On the other hand, it is important to avoid providing recruits with too much information in the screener, because you do not typically want them to come into the groups with preconceived ideas or expectations.

- *Confirmation that the call is not a sales call*—You can help maintain respondent cooperation by reinforcing the idea that this call is only for research purposes and that no sales effort will be made, either during the screening interview or during the focus group itself.

- *Emphasis on confidentiality*—This helps to ensure honest responses. Participants are more likely to be open and comfortable during the screener as well as during the focus group discussion if they are certain that their comments will be held in complete confidentiality.

- ***Industry-sensitive questions***—These questions allow you to avoid biasing the study or giving information to competitors. It is important to ensure that you do not invite direct competitors or anyone potentially able to bias and/or later leak information obtained during the study. You should also screen out persons working for major advertising, public relations, or marketing research firms, who could later provide (even unintentionally) feedback to the competition.

- *Question about recent focus group participation*—This type of question excludes "professional" focus group participants from the groups. With focus groups being such a well-known research methodology, consumers and businesspeople alike are now frequently called on to participate in groups. They are likewise becoming increasingly aware of the co-op fees that accompany these invitations. It is advisable to avoid including participants who have attended such groups so frequently that they tend to run the discussions. Typically, research vendors recommend that contacts should not have participated in a focus group (or at least a group on the same or similar subject matter) within the past six months.

- *Invitation to participate*—This identifies the study as focus group research. Once a contact answers the screening questions and is established as qualified to participate in the study, this phrasing indicates that the respondent is being asked to attend the group.

- *Co-op fee designation*—Typically, as part of the invitation, a specific honorarium is offered to the participant. This is generally expected to entice a recruit to show up as scheduled for the group. As discussed in Chapter 1, the amount typically ranges from $35 to $200 and depends on the topic, location, and the type of participants being recruited.

Recruiting Focus Group Participants

Once the screening questionnaire is developed, the interviewers are briefed on the specific project to be certain that they know exactly the type of person(s) they are looking to recruit. Recruiting generally is conducted approximately two weeks prior to the scheduled first group—early enough to allow for potential problems to occur and be solved, yet not so early that the recruits forget to attend their scheduled sessions! Exceptions to this suggested timing would include, for example, particularly hard-to-recruit participants (such as CEOs or surgeons) or groups where participants need to receive a product to test before they attend the focus groups. (The latter situation is discussed in Chapter 7.) In such cases, it is advisable to begin the recruiting process earlier.

Once the participants are recruited, they will receive a ***confirmation letter***, which acknowledges that they have agreed to participate in the discussion and reiterates the time, date, and co-op fee for their group. In the same mailing, they should also receive detailed directions to the facility where the groups will be conducted. In addition, most research vendors will make ***confirmation calls*** the day prior to the groups to ensure that the participants still plan to attend. These follow-up efforts are the reason why screener questionnaires ask qualified respondents to provide their current mailing address and confirm their telephone number.

During the recruiting process, the moderator and often the client receive ***participant profile matrices*** on an ongoing basis. They should review these as quickly as possible to make sure that the correct participants are being recruited for the correct groups. Typically, the matrix will look somewhat like the one

Table 2-1 Sample Participant Profile Matrix

Credit Union Focus Group Participant Profile

		GROUP 1		
Name	**Banking Decision Maker**	**Age 55+**	**Past Focus Group Participation**	**Industry-Sensitive Responses**
Joan Fritz	Yes	Yes	No	No
Bob Smith	Yes	Yes	No	Yes
Carol Ames	Yes	Yes	No	No
Sue Burns	Yes	No	No	No
Jim Green	Yes	Yes	No	No
Lyn Carr	Yes	Yes	No	No

shown in Table 2-1, which reports the participants recruited for a focus group concerning a credit union senior program.

These matrices allow early cancellation of participants who do not appear to correctly match the preestablished recruitment criteria. Furthermore, they can prove useful if all twelve participants recruited show up for a group and materials (and perhaps facility space) are only designed to accommodate up to ten participants. You can select the ten *best* contacts and release the others (with co-op payments in hand, of course!).

In the example in Table 2-1, the screener questionnaire was based on criteria that participants be a banking services decision maker, be at least fifty-five years old, not work for (or serve on the board of) any related company, and not have attended a focus group during the past six months. However, the initial participant profile matrix shows that Bob Smith does not qualify for the group, as he is somehow affiliated with a designated sensitive industry. Likewise, Sue Burns should be disqualified, as she is not fifty-five or older. Both of these recruits would be recontacted and canceled before they went to the groups (and hence they would *not* be paid the designated co-op fee).

Case Study: Screener Questionnaire Development

Consider another example of screener questionnaire development. Assume, in this case, that you have been asked to develop the screener for a series of focus groups intended to evaluate an airline's new service program. The program is expected to be tiered, with special new services to be offered at airport departure and arrival gates, as well as in flight. Services are expected to be targeted at frequent *coach* fliers in three categories: business, pleasure, and family vacationers with children. The airline is particularly interested in families who travel frequently but typically do not fly. It is believed that these services may attract such people to flights from alternatives such as auto or train travel.

This situation requires you to answer several fundamental questions:

- How would you define the objectives of this study?

- Given your research objectives, which type of focus group would work best for this particular project? Why?

- How would you divide the groups in terms of quotas?

- Once the groups' makeups have been determined, how would the screener questionnaires look for each of the group types?

Try answering the questions on your own before you continue reading.

Definition of Objectives

The overall issue at hand is to determine whether coach fliers will be attracted to the airline's proposed new service program. Objectives are likely to include the following:

- Determine what services currently attract them to their current travel method (air, train, auto, etc.)

- Evaluate targets' interest levels in the proposed new program

- Investigate the likelihood of (1) attracting nonflying travelers with the services; and (2) attracting competitors' frequent-flier customers with the services

- Identify services to add/delete to increase targets' interest levels in the program

You want your objectives to be related to the main purpose of the study. You also want them to be simply defined. Above all, based on these objectives, you will want to identify the best research methodology to use in order to meet these objectives.

Selection of Focus Group Type

Since you are considering a research study to test service *concepts* (and since this is a book on focus group research!), qualitative research would be an appropriate means of meeting your research objectives. Because this is a service program, it is unlikely that there will be any hands-on concept testing. It is more likely that you will present conceptual videos, brochures, and so forth, and then discuss them in the focus group setting.

For this particular type of discussion, the more input you can obtain, the better your analysis will be. A standard eight- to ten-person focus group would be appropriate in this case, as it will allow more bantering of the type that will elicit comments regarding the participants' personal experiences, concerns, and travel needs.

Division of Groups in Terms of Quotas

You know from the preceding project description that you will want to identify frequent coach fliers in each of these categories:

- Business

- Pleasure

- Family vacationers with children

Likewise, you will want to separately identify family vacationers who travel frequently but seldom fly.

Screening for Each Group Type

For each of the preceding categories, you should first list what you will accept as identifiers of people who fall into each group. What criteria will you require? Which criteria will actually determine that a respondent is qualified to participate in one of the focus groups?

For the sake of expediency, we will work through only the business example for the actual screener questionnaire. The process would be similar for the other quota groups. Let's first assume that a few general criteria exist for the business groups. The respondent must meet all of these criteria:

- Travel by coach class when flying for business

- Be traveling *primarily* for business purposes

- Be a member of any frequent-flier program(s)

- Be personally selecting or at least providing input into the airline/flight decision-making process

Based on these criteria, Figure 2-1 presents a suggested screener questionnaire for this particular focus group. This is but one example of how the business fliers' screener questionnaire could look. Note that in this sample, questions S5 through S8 were not asked merely to provide additional information regarding potential participants. Rather, by asking these four brief questions, if we were to find out that the participant does not qualify for the business group or if he or she is unable to attend that group, he or she could possibly fit the profile for the family travel or pleasure travel groups and be transferred into one of those groups accordingly. Attention to such details can save time and money during your recruiting efforts.

FIGURE 2-1 Suggested Screener Questionnaire for Case Study

Frequent Flier Service Study (Business Fliers) Focus Group Screener

Date: __ __/__ __/__ __Interviewer ID #: __ __ __ __

[Ask to speak with male or female head of household who is currently employed.]

Hello, my name is _____ with ABC Research in Anytown. We are conducting a brief research study with business travelers. We are not selling anything and will only take a few minutes of your time. [If respondent advises he or she is not a business traveler, ask if anyone else in house is. If yes, transfer or arrange callback; otherwise, thank and terminate.]

S1. Do you travel for business purposes in your current job?

　　1. Yes [continue to **S2**]

　　2. No [check re: other in household; otherwise skip to **S5**]

　　3. Unemployed [thank and terminate]

　　4. Don't know/refused [thank and terminate]

S2. On average, how many business flights per year do you take? [record one only]

　　1. None/don't fly on business [skip to **S5**]

2. 1 to 9 [skip to **S5**]

3. 10 to 15 [continue to **S3**]

4. 16 to 20 [continue to **S3**]

5. 21 or more [continue to **S3**]

6. Don't know [ask for best estimate; otherwise, thank and terminate]

7. Refused [thank and terminate]

S3. And, when on business flights, which class of flight service do you most frequently fly in? [read list and record one only]

1. Coach [continue to **S4**]

2. Business/connoisseur/executive [continue to **S4**]

3. First class [continue to **S4**]

4. Don't know/refused [thank and terminate]

5. Not applicable—noncommercial plane or corporate plane [continue to **S4**]

S4. Do you or does anyone in your immediate family work for an advertising agency, airline, airport, or travel agency?

1. Yes [thank and terminate]

2. No [continue to **S5**]

3. Don't know/refused [thank and terminate]

S5. (In addition to your business travel), do you ever fly for pleasure such as on vacations?

    1. Yes [continue to **S6**]

    2. No [skip to **S9**]

    3. Don't know/refused [thank and terminate]

S6. When flying for pleasure, which class do you typically fly in? [record one only]

    1. Coach [continue to **S7**]

    2. Business/connoisseur/executive [skip to **S9**]

    3. First class [skip to **S9**]

    4. Don't know/refused [thank and terminate]

S7. Approximately how many flights do you take per year for pleasure?

    Record estimated #: __ __ __

S8. And when you fly for pleasure, who, if anyone, typically accompanies you? [do not read list; record all that apply]

    1. No one; travel alone

    2. Spouse/partner

    3. Friend

    4. Children

    5. Other relative

6. Other [specify:_____]

7. Don't know/refused

S9. Do you currently belong to any airlines' frequent-flier programs?

1. Yes [specify: _____]

2. No

3. Don't know/refused

S10. Participants qualify as follows (and in this order):

First qualify business fliers: **S3 = 1; S4 = 2; S9 = 1**

If not, then pleasure (no kids): **S5 = 1; S6 = 1; S7 = 2+; S8 not = 4 and S9 = 1**

If not, then pleasure with kids: **S5 = 1; S6 = 1; S7 = 2+; S8 = 4; S9 = 1**

Invitation:

ABC Research will be conducting a focus group discussion with frequent fliers such as yourself. The discussion will center on new services for frequent fliers. The purpose of the group is solely to obtain your opinions, and all of your comments will be kept confidential. The session will last approximately 90 minutes, and you will receive [Business = $100; Pleasure = $45] for your participation. Would you be interested in attending this group?

1. Yes [schedule for appropriate group]

2. No [thank and terminate]

3. Don't know/refused [thank and terminate]

[Insert the dates and times of the groups to allow the recruiters to schedule the participants.]

Participant Information:

So that we can send you a confirmation letter and directions to the group, I need your full name and the appropriate mailing address. [Business only: I also need your position/title.]

Name: _____

Title: _____

Company: _____

Business Address: _____

City: _____ State: _____ Zip: _____

Also, I would like to confirm that the phone number I reached you at is:

[Read number from sample and record or correct it below. Add extension if applicable.]

(__ __ __) __ __ __-__ __ __ __ [Ext: __ __ __ __]

Thank you for your time! We look forward to seeing you at [time/date scheduled].

The Discussion Guide

Once the focus group participants are targeted, the discussion guide needs to be developed. This book will look at the discussion guide in two separate contexts; first, how to *develop* a good discussion guide and then, in Chapter 4, how to *use* the discussion guide when moderating groups. Appendix B also provides additional examples of discussion guides.

The discussion guide (also called the moderator's guide) can be developed at any point before the start of the first group session, but it is preferable to allow adequate time for review of the discussion guide by all parties associated with the design of the research project. There are often changes to the flow of the outline, additional questions that arise, and other issues that may require revisions. It is better to take these into consideration well in advance to avoid last-minute confusion.

The focus group discussion guide is an outline the moderator follows when conducting the focus groups. It ensures that the focus group discussion thoroughly covers all the necessary topics. These topics are based on the research objectives, which are the basis for the study, as discussed in Chapter 1.

To better illustrate the development of a discussion guide, consider the following example. A high-technology company has developed a software product that, most simply described, provides inbound/outbound telephone customer service–related operators with enhanced capabilities for handling their calls. The company wants to test user perceptions regarding the product prototype to meet a set of predefined objectives. The firm has three objectives:

1. Identify the most important features for users

2. Measure usability compared to competitive systems

3. Evaluate potential add-on features needed to fine-tune the product

To obtain the most objective overall results, the client company agrees that it is best to conduct focus groups with its competitors' customers as well as its own. In many cases, this decision might require two discussion guides, one for customers and one for competitive customers, but this is not the case for this particular project. Figure 2-2 shows a suggested focus group discussion guide for the study.

FIGURE 2-2 Suggested Software Focus Group Discussion
Guide

Software Focus Group Discussion Guide

(5 min.) Introduction

- Greeting

- Purpose of focus groups

  - Opportunity to provide input about a new software
    program that assists in outbound and inbound calling,
    such as the types of calls you typically deal with in
    your positions

- Ground rules

  - Role of moderator

  - Recording equipment and one-way mirror

  - Confidentiality of comments/responses

  - Individual opinions (no right or wrong)

  - Speak one at a time and as clearly as possible

- Brief get-acquainted period

  - Participants' names, positions, companies, PC
    experience

(10 min.) Current System Software

- What kinds of calls do they make (sales, collections, etc.)?

    - If collections, for what type of accounts?

    - If sales, does system prompt them regarding how to handle objections?

- Will system generate letters/faxes for them?

- How is the information (used to talk with customers) accessed? (Does it come up on their screen, or do they have to press keys to get to it?)

- Number of calls they personally handle per shift (inbound vs. outbound)

- Likes and dislikes about current system (i.e., speed, user-friendliness, ease of use, particular features)

- How long did it take them to learn their current system?

- Any changes that would make their system easier to use

(15 min.) Product Demo/Brief Question-and-Answer Session

(10 min.) Initial Evaluation

- Based on demo, what do they see that they like/dislike about product?

- Initially, how would they feel about using this system versus their current one?

(15 min.) Hands-On Trial

- Participants try out product and get a feel for it.

(10 min.) General Usability

- How user-friendly is this program?

- Based on the trial, how does it compare in terms of usability to their current systems?

- Likes and dislikes regarding ease of use

(25 min.) Feature Evaluation

- What are the standout features—those they would definitely use?

- Are there features they would not use or not require in their own situations?

- Are there any features that would be useful provided they were changed in some manner?

- Specific features

    - Icons

    - Help capabilities

    - Screen layouts

(5 min.) Closing Comments

- Any additional comments?

- Thank participants and remind them to pick up co-op fees on way out.

Case Study: Discussion Guide Development

Let's continue the airline service program study discussed earlier in this chapter. Referring to the initial objectives of that study, try to draft a discussion guide for the quota group consisting of family vacationers with children who do not fly frequently. (For additional practice, you may want to attempt drafts for a second quota group as well.)

Once you have prepared your own version of the outline, review the suggested outline for the guide in Figure 2-3.

FIGURE 2-3 Suggested Discussion Guide for Case Study

Airline Focus Group Family Vacationers Discussion Guide Draft

(10 min.) Introduction

- Greeting

- Purpose of focus groups

- Ground rules

  - Role of moderator

  - Recording equipment and one-way mirror

  - Confidentiality of comments/responses

  - Individual opinions (no right or wrong answers)

  - Speak one at a time and as clearly as possible

- Icebreaker exercise

- Participants' names, number of children, favorite vacation destination

(15 min.) Travel Experiences

- You have indicated that you do *not* typically fly for vacations: what is your preferred means of travel on family vacations? [probe: train, car, cruise, etc.]

- Why?

- Why do you choose *not* to fly? [probe: past bad experiences on airline? perceived cost? other?]

(45 min.) New Service Concepts

- Introduction: A major airline is considering potential services designed specifically for families traveling by air. We would like your opinions regarding these services.

- Presentation of service concepts

- Ask for each concept (5 in all):

  - Likes and dislikes? Why? Suggested improvements?

  - Would you use this when traveling with your own family? Why/why not?

  - Do you have similar services available to you now when you travel by [current mode of transportation]? If yes, describe.

(15 min.) Potential Effects of Services

- Assuming that each of the concepts you favored were available on an airline today, would you be more likely to fly than go by [current mode of transportation]? Why/why not?

- Which airline would you expect to offer these services? Why?

- Would you expect to pay less, the same as current fares, or more in order to have these services included in your fares? Why?

(5 min.) Closing Comments

- Final suggestions/comments?

- Remind participants to get co-op fees at front desk.

Who you select to participate in your focus group, how you recruit them, and what you discuss with them will determine how well you are able to answer the questions you identified in your research objectives. How smoothly these discussions run, however, depends a great deal on the facilities you select for your groups. The next chapter will address this topic.

CHAPTER

3

Facility Issues

The focus group facility plays an important role in the research process. It is important to select a facility that is conveniently located to your target audience. In addition, the facility must be comfortable or your participants are likely to be ill at ease during the discussion. And certain standard requirements such as a moderation communication system and audio- and videotaping capabilities should be met to ensure smooth moderating and accurate reporting. This chapter deals with these aspects of the focus group study.

Selecting a Research Facility

There are typically two ways to select a research facility for a focus group study. First, you may look for each individual facility, despite the number of groups and cities, on your own and make reservations for the facilities accordingly. This is most often the case for the research vendor's project manager, who coordinates all aspects of the client's study. A nonresearcher more often will rely on a contracted marketing research vendor to identify the best facilities in the areas where the groups will be conducted. If you are looking for vendors yourself, potential resources include references from colleagues, the yellow pages, and annual publications such as *The American Marketing Association International Marketing Services Guide*, the *AMA Green Book (International Directory of Marketing Research Companies & Services)*, and *Quirk's Marketing Research Review*.

However you make the selection, it is helpful to look for certain qualities in the facilities you consider for your project. The basic criteria to consider when selecting a focus group facility are listed in Table 3-1.

Table 3-1 Criteria for Selecting a Focus Group Facility

Reputation and experience

Recruiting capabilities

Accessibility to participants

Parking availability

Alternative facilities available in the same area

Focus group room size and availability

Audio- and videotaping capabilities

Viewing room arrangement and capacity

Moderator and viewer communication system

Test kitchen facilities (if the groups require taste-testing of food or beverage products)

Availability of electrical outlets (particularly if electronic equipment is expected to be used in the room)

Availability of any group-related tools (such as computers, whiteboard, flip charts, VCRs)

Refreshment options for participants and clients

Host(ess) services

Each of these factors should play a role in the selection of a focus group facility, but the most important aspect of your decision is the reputation of the firm.

Ask the vendor for client references, and call each of them before finalizing a schedule with the facility. Questions you should ask references include the comfort level of the rooms, professionalism of the staff, problem areas to expect with the facility (if they had to cite one), and quality of the firm's recruiting efforts.

Even if you are only looking for a room because recruiting is to be done through a centralized site, it may be useful for future projects to have a recruiting reference as well. Recruiting (the screening interview process) is potentially the most crucial aspect of your focus group research. When selecting a vendor, it is important to identify how many interviewers the staff will have available for your project and what they anticipate the recruiting time line to be. In addition, will they assist you in developing the best possible screener questionnaire, and do they typically confirm recruits before the groups? It is also helpful to know their procedure for replacing recruits who drop out prior to the groups.

The geographic location of the facility is also important. Downtown facilities may prove perfect for attracting business-people for groups immediately following their workday. They can, however, prove nerve-racking for the suburbanite attempting to locate the group site in rush-hour traffic. Plan for your groups accordingly. Easy access is important, as is adequate (and preferably free) parking. If your participants have to fight their way into a parking lot to attend your group, they may simply opt to leave rather than hassling with the situation.

The research experience and reputation as well as the general convenience of the research facility are all crucial to the success of a focus group project. Certain other details from Table 3-1, although seemingly mundane, do need to be taken into consideration. Some of these items are covered in the following sections.

Room Availability and Size

It is important to ensure that the facility where the focus groups will be conducted has a room available for the dates required. Be clear in your request for daytime and/or evening groups. Typically, participant attendance is better in evening groups.

In addition, it is important to confirm that the focus group room you have reserved meets the needs of the group(s) that are scheduled. For instance, assume you have arranged for twelve recruits, expecting that several may cancel or not show up at all. You may be surprised when all twelve recruits arrive as scheduled. Should you choose to allow all twelve to participate, will the room comfortably accommodate all of them? Will the moderator be able to move around easily in the room without obstructions? Is there enough food, test product, and so forth available? If the participants and/or the moderator are uncomfortable, the quality of the discussion is likely to suffer.

If you are unable to personally check out the focus group room, take precautions to ensure that it will meet your needs. Ask to see a diagram of the room layout with measurements indicated if possible. Many focus group facilities offer this information as part of their marketing materials. You might also contact references for the facility to get their impressions of the rooms offered at a specific facility.

Viewing Room Capacity

The clients and other attendees require adequate space to observe the focus groups from a *viewing room*. From a practical standpoint, it is advisable to limit the number of clients viewing in order to keep background noise in this room to a minimum. After determining the number of viewers, confirm that adequate seating will be available.

In addition, you should inquire about the level of soundproofing between the viewing room and the focus group room. Thin walls limit your discussion opportunities while watching the groups. While background talk should, of course, be kept at a minimum to get the most value from the groups, you should still be able to discuss unexpected issues, note similarities between groups, and so forth without fear of disrupting the focus group discussion.

Other items to check on include provisions for desk space, availability of an outside phone line, placement of electrical outlets, and whether viewing is provided via mirror, monitor, or both. Also ask how seating is arranged. Tiered seating provides maximum viewing when several clients are watching the groups.

Immediately prior to the start of your groups, you should test the visibility of the focus group room from the client viewing room. Are you able to clearly see all of the boards, prototypes, etc., that will need to be caught on the videotape? If you cannot see them, it is possible that the video will not pick them all up either. In addition, you will want to ensure that the viewers will be able to see all of the participants' faces. Positioning of the moderator is important. Typically, the moderator's back is to the viewers to allow clients (and the camera) to pick up participants' body language and assess their initial reactions to a comment or idea.

Host(ess) Services

Typically, the cost of the facility rental includes the services of a focus group *host(ess)*. This is far from a frivolous add-on. If the facility does not offer these services, you should request them.

The host(ess) serves as the liaison between the viewers and

the moderator, delivering notes to the moderator. In addition, he or she ensures that the viewers are comfortable in terms of refreshments, room temperature controls, and the viewing room audio levels. Typically, this person also handles the audio- and videotaping procedures, as well as any additional needs related to conducting the groups, such as setting up a VCR or obtaining flip charts.

Moderator Communication System

The viewers' means of communicating with the moderator is usually the host(ess). When viewers have a question or want to recommend additional probing, the host or hostess takes a note directly into the focus group session. The moderator will then incorporate the comment or query into the conversation. There are, however, occasionally other modes of communication between the moderator and viewers. Depending on your preferences, you should confirm the method being used by a particular facility.

One option, although infrequently utilized, is for the moderator to wear an earpiece that allows immediate communication from the viewers to the moderator. While the apparent high tech nature of this option might seem appealing to the clients, it can be extremely distracting for the moderator, thereby causing distractions and interruptions to the established flow of the discussion. Another communications arrangement is for the moderator to take one or two extremely brief breaks during the course of a group, typically while participants are otherwise occupied (such as during a written exercise) and then just before releasing the respondents at the end of the group. This allows viewers to give ongoing input to the moderator, while the moderator can determine when breaks in the discussion will cause the least disruption to the conversation.

Viewers and the moderator should agree in advance on how they should communicate. This avoids unnecessary confusion during the groups. Appointing one viewer to be in charge of providing input to the moderator maintains a fast and efficient flow of communication.

Frequently, the participants will make comments while the moderator is out of the room. These unaided comments can prove to be useful when later reviewed on video- or audiotapes.

Audio- and Videotaping Capabilities

When selecting a facility for focus groups, it is also important to take into account the facilities' recording capabilities. In-person focus groups should be videotaped in order to record nuances such as facial expressions, attitudes, and interactions. For other group types, such as telefocus groups, you should ensure that audiotaping is available.

For in-person groups, using both audio- and videotaping provides "insurance" that your groups will be recorded. For instance, it is not unusual for the sound on focus group tapes to occasionally have static. If one taping method or the other fails, there is still a backup for reporting purposes. In all cases, audio- and videotaping equipment should be tested *before* the start of your initial focus group session at each facility. Tests should be done when enough time remains to make any necessary adjustments to the equipment.

In terms of videotaping, there are typically two options for the client: *stand-alone video* versus the services of a professional video operator. Stand-alone videotaping is generally the most cost-effective option. It involves the use of the focus group facility's (typically) wall-mounted video camera. When properly set, this should provide a complete view of the moderator and all participants in the room. A stand-alone video should generally suffice unless there are complications that would require a camera operator's expertise. Possible complications include a great deal of movement during the groups, visuals that need to be clearly caught on video, or an odd-shaped conference room or table. For instance, if you were testing a product that involves hands-on evaluation by the participants, the ability to more closely observe a given participant in action would be important. Other situations that would warrant a video operator would be certain advertising tests. It can be beneficial to be able to pan in on focus group participants' initial reactions when viewing advertisements for the first time. Finally, if a facility's equipment appears outdated and facility options are limited, it would be advisable to seek the services of a professional videotaping service rather than to rely on less-than-effective taping by the facility.

Audiovisual Equipment

Place requests ahead of time for any audiovisual equipment or other tools the moderator and/or participants will be expected to utilize during the focus group sessions. Examples of the types of equipment and tools that might be required in focus groups include the following:

- VCRs

- Televisions

- Cassette players

- Whiteboards and/or flip charts

- Overhead and/or slide projectors

- Computer equipment (including PCs and printers)

- Notepads and writing utensils (usually for participants)

- Bulletin boards or other means of hanging materials on walls

These are, of course, just some possible examples, and the list does not include items that may be tested during the groups.

As with the taping equipment, it is advisable to test any electronic equipment in advance of the groups.

While the facility you select is an important factor in your project, more crucial still is the assurance that the groups will be conducted correctly. The following chapter deals with focus group moderating.

Focus Group Moderation

Unbiased and professional moderating is key to meeting focus groups' objectives. Moderating is a practiced skill, and a moderator can make or break the entire research project. This chapter deals with how to select a moderator as well as how to use the discussion guide and moderating techniques in the course of a focus group project.

Selecting a Moderator

A crucial aspect of ensuring successful focus groups is selecting the right moderator for the project. Focus group moderating may appear to be easy, but it requires a great deal of skill. Above all, it is preferable to select a professional research moderator who has conducted numerous groups in the same field as yours or in similar industries.

Using professional research moderators prevents the bias that can be present if you conduct the groups yourself. Marketers inevitably have some preferred outcome to the study, while the independent moderator does not. Indeed, professional moderators are even superior to the moderating services of most university professors, because many professors lack the practical business experience required in order to relate to certain participants and analyze the focus group results.

Skills of the Moderator

Insist on references, and be sure to call the references provided to get their input prior to selecting your group moderator. Ask these contacts about the prospective moderator's organizational and time management skills, flexibility, control of the groups, and ability to probe on issues pertinent to the client's objectives.

Even if the moderator's references are impeccable, if time allows, request a video sample to allow you to see the moderator in action. No vendor will provide you with a poor reference! Viewing some of the moderator's work allows you to get a realistic viewpoint. How well does the moderator cover the material in the time allotted? Is he or she able to respond to client notes over the course of the group or work with changes made between sessions? Is he or she strong enough to remain unbiased and insist that changes not be made if they could adversely affect the nature of the project? Is he or she able to control the group if there is either a very strong-willed or an extremely introverted participant? Does he or she know when to probe and when to let a subject drop in order to continue on with the discussion?

These are all important qualities in a moderator. The best moderators know when to be quiet and let the conversation flow and when it is necessary to take control and steer participants back on track.

Table 4-1 provides a comprehensive checklist of qualities you should look for in a focus group moderator. Let's briefly discuss each of these qualities.

Table 4-1 Qualities of a Good Moderator

Ability to learn quickly

Experience

Organizational skills

Flexiblility

Good memory

Good listening skills

Strong probing skills

Time management skills

Good personality

- *Ability to learn quickly*—The moderator must be a quick study, with the ability to comprehend even complicated or highly technical concepts in a brief time, then relay these ideas in a group without confusing the participants.

- *Experience*—It is best to use a moderator who has conducted many focus groups, preferably in your industry, because less of a learning curve will be involved in the briefing.

- *Organizational skills*—A moderator should be prepared to start the groups on time and be familiar with the related discussion guides, prototypes to be tested, and so on. He or she must be able to stick to a schedule and meet preestablished deadlines.

- *Flexibility*—The moderator should be able to adjust quickly to changes in the discussion guide(s) and be comfortable and able to deal with notes sent in by clients during the focus groups.

- *Good memory*—A moderator should be able to remember all aspects of the discussion guide so that comments brought up early in a group can be dealt with during the natural flow of the conversation. In addition, he or she should be able to recall comments made throughout the course of the discussion in order to be able to refer back to them as needed during the group.

- *Good listening skills*—The moderator should concentrate on what is being said in order to tie comments together as appropriate. If he or she takes copious notes during the groups, the conversation will not flow as naturally, so this should be discouraged. (This is what videotaping is intended for!) The moderator should also clarify comments when their meaning is not completely clear.

- *Strong probing skills*—A good moderator knows the difference between probing the focus group participants and leading them. When a participant makes an insightful comment and then trails off without providing adequate explanation, the moderator should, for instance, ask why the participant feels that way. On the other hand, he or she should not put words into the participant's mouth by saying, for example, "So you feel that way because product X doesn't taste as good as product Y?" when the participant has not indicated any specific reason for the initial response. The moderator's job is not to second-guess the participants, but rather to delve deeper and encourage them to express their own feelings with greater clarity.

- *Time management skills*—Moderating involves tight deadlines. Each group has a preset time line, usually between ninety minutes and two hours. During this time, it is the moderator's responsibility to cover all of the items in the discussion guide as thoroughly as possible. A strong moderator will be able to manage his or her time well during the groups, probing when it is most important and cutting off side conversations that do not really pertain to the objectives of the study to avoid slowing the pace of the discussion.

- *Good personality*—The best moderators are comfortable being in groups and can make others comfortable as well. They develop a rapport with the focus group participants quickly at the start of the session and maintain it throughout the discussion. They are patient with participants who are arrogant, and they can engage even the shy attendees in the conversation.

Other Considerations

Along with these skills, a few other considerations define the desirability of the moderator. First, most situations call for the moderator to dress professionally, even if the participants are wearing jeans. This adds to the image of the group as being professionally run and providing important results. It also further establishes the moderator as the person "in charge."

In some specialized cases, the gender of the moderator may also be a concern. For instance, if a medical focus group discussion is centered around prostate cancer, men may feel far more comfortable with a male moderator and be more willing to discuss the topic. Likewise, most women participating in a focus group concerning a new feminine hygiene product would probably prefer a female moderator. Although a skilled professional moderator of either sex has the ability to cover these topics, participants tend to react more openly regarding sensitive or highly personal issues when the moderator is of their own gender.

The moderator should be considered a member of the client's marketing research team, so the moderator you choose should be a team player. If a candidate for the job is abrasive and/or uncooperative, consider another moderator. These qualities may be apparent to the focus group participants as well and therefore interfere with the discussion. The moderator should provide your team with good research and not simply agree with you to keep you happy. He or she should, however, be able to explain why he or she may disagree with the project team's interpretations of the discussion.

Occasionally, a vendor may suggest that a *co-moderator* be used for a specific focus group project. This assistance can be useful if you have to cover a detailed topic that includes hands-on demonstrations. Likewise, it can be helpful if the moderator and co-moderator play off each other well. Such interactions can provide the added benefit of putting all participants at ease, as the participants can usually identify easily with at least one of the two moderators. Nevertheless, this process should be discouraged if it appears to be suggested primarily for the benefit of the research vendor, such as using your groups as training sessions for a novice moderator. Even if the vendor advises that the second moderator will be provided at no additional cost, this process can slow your groups' pace (even with an excellent lead moderator). You should therefore decline the "offer."

Use of the Discussion Guide

Chapter 1 identified the screener questionnaire as the most important tool in the focus group research study. Closely following the screener in importance is the moderator's discussion guide. The discussion guide serves as a detailed outline for the moderator to use in leading the focus group discussion. The development of the discussion guide was discussed in detail in Chapter 2. Here the discussion concerns how the moderator should use the discussion guide.

Just as focus group moderators' styles vary, so do their preferred discussion guide formats. Some moderators may prefer a formal outline style, while others lean toward a simple bullet list of general topics to cover. Occasionally, moderators may opt to use a discussion guide that lists extremely detailed questions, almost in an actual questionnaire format. However, this type of moderator's guide can discourage the spontaneity and flexibility that are so important to the success of the focus group discussion.

Regardless of the exact style used, the discussion guide provides a proposed framework for the discussion. *Framework* is the key word here. The discussion guide (as well as the moderator) needs to be flexible. The purpose of qualitative research is to establish an open flow of input from the participants. If the moderator is rigid and does not allow participants to stray from the precise ordering of discussion topics, certain ideas may not even develop and important comments may get lost forever. If, however, the moderator allows conversations related to the overall group subject matter to occur in a natural sequence, less aided input may be required, and comments will not be at risk of being lost by being put on hold until they "fit" into the outline.

While it is important to maintain the general flow and focus of the discussion guide throughout all of the groups conducted in a given study, frequently the guide may be modified from group to group. This allows the moderator to incorporate ideas that were not previously considered but arose during the course of the initial groups.

Several examples of moderators' focus group discussion guides appear in Appendix B.

Moderator's Attention Level

Not only must the moderator be flexible, but he or she must also be constantly aware of the participants' comments. Are the participants on track, or have they lost sight of the subject matter? If a comment seems to be related to the topic but was not originally in the discussion guide, the moderator should weigh its importance and pertinence. Does the unexpected issue warrant more detailed probing?

To determine the relevance of an issue, the moderator should consider the following questions:

- Is the new issue directly related to the overall focus of the discussion?

- Will this issue better enable the client to meet the study's objectives?

- Are others in the group latching onto this issue? Will a discussion develop, or will it allow one outgoing individual to take the platform?

If the answer to all of the preceding questions is yes, it is typically a good idea to proceed with the additional topic. If the subject is not directly related to the study or not directly tied to the objectives, the group could be derailed by allowing detailed discussion of it. The moderator needs to remain aware of the objectives throughout each group.

Also related to paying attention is the need for the moderator to be aware of each comment made. As noted earlier, if a comment pertains to a later topic in the discussion guide, it is usually better to cover the topic when it comes up naturally in the flow of the conversation. If unrelated issues arise, the moderator should discourage further conversation regarding them. Paying close attention to comments also helps the moderator determine the best use of probing questions asked to clarify participants' views or to stimulate further discussion of a specific comment.

Finally, while it is not encouraged, the discussion guide is frequently changed during the course of the groups. Either the moderator or sponsor of the groups may note additional issues that should be covered in the remaining groups. Likewise, they may determine that the recruited participants simply are unable to actively discuss certain issues. For instance, they may lack knowledge, responsibility, or experience needed to discuss a topic with the necessary detail. Such changes may occur during a group via a note to the moderator, but they more often occur in a debriefing session following one of the groups. Changes to the discussion guide should only be made when they are ascertained to provide value to the study in terms of the preestablished research objectives.

Introducing Participants to Focus Group Procedures

Before starting the actual focus group discussion, even prior to introductions, the moderator should advise participants that the groups are being video- and/or audiotaped. If any participant objects, that person should be released from the group without argument. Whether or not the departing recruit receives co-op payments for coming to the location may vary by situation. For reasons of goodwill, it is advisable to pay the co-op fee if the client has already been identified to participants. Note that a very small percentage of focus group recruits are ever concerned with the recording aspect of such studies.

Likewise, the moderator must call participants' attention to the fact that people are viewing the group, either from behind the one-way mirror or via camera. Again, this is seldom an issue, and once the discussion is in progress, participants seldom give the mirror a second glance. The viewers do not necessarily have to be identified as being affiliated with a specific company. Typically, the moderator will simply note that "members of the research team" are viewing to help with note taking or that the study's "sponsor" is viewing the groups. Both statements are truthful without compromising the unbiased nature of the discussion.

Along with these issues, the moderator should also stress certain standard ground rules of the focus group discussion process:

- The moderator's role

- Speaking clearly and one at a time

- No right or wrong answers

- Need for active participation

- Breaking the ice

Moderator's Role

The moderator's role is to keep the focus group discussion on track. The discussion guide will provide the tool with which he or she can do this, allowing discussion on topics indicated on the guide at any point, but not allowing side topics to develop unless they appear relevant to the overall objectives of the study. Overly enthusiastic participants need to be reined in politely, while those who shrink back from participating should firmly be encouraged to offer their opinions.

In addition, the moderator should put the participants at ease. A good rapport with the participants will lead to more candid responses. One way to do this is to use first names, rather than "Mr." or "Ms.," because it puts all participants on the same level during the discussion.

Speaking Clearly and One at a Time

It is important that the moderator instruct the participants to speak clearly and one at a time. The most important reason is that it allows the moderator to better hear all input and properly probe on pertinent comments. In addition, it prevents a noisy jumble of comments from being picked up on the audio- or videotapes. Finally, it provides for a better rapport among the group participants; each respectfully listening to what the others say.

No Right and Wrong Answers

It is important for the moderator to emphasize for respondents that there are no right or wrong responses during the course of the focus groups. Participants should be encouraged to express their own ideas and opinions without feeling that others will disagree or be argumentative.

Need for Active Participation

The moderator must make participants aware of how important their input is to the overall objectives of the study. They should be encouraged to talk on each topic discussed. To encourage participation, the moderator should frequently use participants' names and alternate between respondents when asking for comments.

Breaking the Ice

During the brief overall introduction of the focus group methodology to the group, the moderator will often implement one of a variety of ice-breaking techniques to relax respondents and start the flow of conversation. In addition to asking participants to introduce themselves, the moderator typically asks one of a variety of questions to set the pace for the group. It is best to tie this question directly to the subject matter, as in the following examples for consumer groups:

- Travel topic—favorite vacation spot

- Retail topic—favorite place to shop for a related product

Conducting the Focus Group Discussion

Following the icebreaker, the moderator moves the group into the main discussion. The professional moderator's repertoire includes a variety of tactics for keeping the discussion moving and on track.

Maintaining Control of Group Discussions

In an ideal focus group situation, the participants should be talking mainly with each other, rather than to the moderator. Still, despite the request that participants speak one at a time, invariably side conversations occur during the course of a focus group. It is the moderator's responsibility to curb these conversations without discouraging input. Methods include asking interrupters to "hold their thought for a moment" or simply by issuing a casual reminder that the videotapes will be jumbled with overlapping comments, so it is important to speak one at a time.

Keeping the Conversation on Track

The moderator cannot allow issues to get confused during the course of the group's discussion. While the focus group methodology encourages free-flowing conversation, there is still an overriding main topic. The group must adhere to this guiding topic in order to avoid losing the value of the research, and it is the moderator's job to refocus participants if they wander too far off course.

Moderation Techniques and Approaches

While the focus group conversation is not necessarily expected to follow the precise order designated in the discussion guide, there is a definite need for the moderator to get to the information that will answer the clients' business questions. The moderator generally goes into a group knowing some general information about the participants based on the participant profile matrix (discussed in Chapter 2). In some cases, participants may also be asked to complete brief questionnaires prior to the start of the group to embellish on their experience and qualifications (see Chapter 5). Although these "survey" results are not quantitative, they may later help to clarify a participant's reactions and provide greater depth in the reporting stage.

It is as important for the moderator to observe what is *not* verbalized during the course of the conversation as what the participants are actually saying. One participant may voice great dislike for an idea, while another may simply sit back, smile slightly, and shake her head. While she did not speak up directly, she obviously expressed disagreement with the other participant. The moderator should pick up on this type of disagreement and seek to have the opposing opinion noted: "Jean, you seemed to disagree with Bob's last comment. Could you tell us why?" The moderator needs to keep the atmosphere nonconfrontational while still encouraging participants to openly express differences of opinions.

It is, as noted earlier, the moderator's role to keep the discussion moving without constantly being the main speaker during the group. Probing questions and clarification of participants' responses are valuable, but they do not necessarily keep a conversation alive! Moderators therefore use a wide variety of techniques to draw out thoughtful, useful information from participants. As this book is not intended as a moderator's training manual, this discussion briefly introduces only a few of these as examples. They are simple polling or ranking exercises, comparison games, role-playing, and the informal technique of taking a break to allow for unaided insights.

Polling or Ranking Exercises

A moderator typically uses polling exercises to get a feeling for participants' top one or two choices among a number of items. The moderator will want to obtain a consensus from participants, such as in the comparison of several aspects of a new airline program, as in the case in Chapter 2. Assume, for example, that the moderator has listed on a flip chart five possible services that an airline is considering offering to business travelers flying in coach class. All five services have been described in detail and discussed with the participants. Now the moderator wants to find out the top two services that participants would use. He asks them to "cast their votes" for the top two and indicates the tally of the "poll" alongside each service listed.

Another method used for this type of exercise is ranking. This works best with a brief list of items (five or fewer). In the preceding example, each participant would be asked to apply a rank (one to five) to each service listed. Simpler still would be to rank their top three choices. This would help to produce a picture of participants' overall preferences. Again, remember that these are qualitative responses, *not* quantitative.

Comparison Games

In some cases, it may be difficult for participants to adequately describe how they feel about a certain product or company. For example, if someone asked you to describe your car, you might note its model and make, its color, and the number of doors it has. For the moderator, however, that is not necessarily enough! He wants to know how you *feel* about the car. To get to this level of description, comparison-type "games" are often used to obtain a more emotional picture.

In this example, the moderator would ask you (the participant) to describe your car as a person. Is it upper or middle class? Where does it like to travel? What are its hobbies? What type of clothes does it wear? What is its favorite sport? These types of questions bring the description to a different level, one that the moderator can use in evaluating how a participant feels about a product.

Role-Playing

Another technique that helps "paint a picture" for the moderator is role-playing. The moderator may, for instance, ask participants to act out with each other a sales process, with one trying to identify the features and sell the product being discussed in the group to the others. This can help by showing what the participants really see as the strong selling points of the product. Ultimately, this process will also be useful in evaluating the focus group results.

Break in the Session

Another "trick" that is quite effective, particularly with new product focus groups, is to take a very brief break after the concepts have been presented or key materials shown. The benefits of this are twofold. First, it allows the moderator to touch base with the clients to obtain any crucial inputs they might wish to provide. Probably even more useful are the discussions that can arise while the moderator is out of the room. Frequently, the participants begin to discuss concepts on their own, providing unaided insights that are fresh at that point in the group.

Moderators have developed various techniques that they have found successful in conducting focus groups. It would be impossible to include all of them here, but the key to any technique's success is ensuring that it is unbiased in its approach. Bias can be introduced in many ways, including question wording, notes sent in by viewers, and reactions from the moderator to certain responses. It is important to prevent this from occurring to ensure that the results of the study are reliable. The next chapter deals with the evaluation of focus group results.

Focus Group Evaluation

Ultimately, the conclusions drawn from the focus groups are generally presented in some form of report. It is this report that the research clients will use in their decision-making process. This chapter provides an overview of how the qualitative results of a focus group study can be compiled into a report with actionable recommendations.

Writing the Report

Typically, a focus group study concludes with the delivery and presentation of a final report, which summarizes the qualitative findings of a series of groups. Whether or not the client believes that it is necessary, he or she really does need this *executive summary report*. This documentation pulls together the similarities and differences between the groups and ties the findings back to the overall research objectives of the study. While a focus group report will probably never provide a single final solution, it should prove to be a useful decision-making tool.

As noted earlier, the moderator usually conducts the research analysis of the focus group study. This situation is, of course, preferable, given that the moderator is expected to have been thoroughly briefed on the study's objectives. In addition, the moderator has personally interacted with each of the focus group participants, giving him or her the most in-depth perspective of the discussions to be evaluated.

There are, however, exceptions to the "moderator as analyst" rule. For instance, in many cases, particularly in international focus group research, more than one moderator may be involved in a given study. This could, for example, occur with a number of groups being held in the United States, the United Kingdom, France, and Germany. While the American moderator would likely also moderate the groups in the United Kingdom, it is just as likely that other native-speaking moderators would be required to take over these duties in France and Germany. As the reporting phase of the study begins, the report (and often the related presentation) in such a case is likely to involve a collaboration of the efforts of all moderators involved in the study.

In a similar situation, although occurring less frequently, co-moderators may jointly conduct focus group discussions. In such a case, as with an international moderating team, the pair of moderators would generally combine efforts to analyze the results of the qualitative study.

While the moderator tends to be the best analyst for focus group research, it is not uncommon for another member of the marketing research vendor's staff to take over the responsibility of analysis. To best accomplish reporting in this situation, the analyst should have attended, if not all, at least a number of the groups personally, viewed the remainder on tape, read transcripts (if applicable), and taken notes as well. It is also preferable that the person writing the focus group report has participated in the final debriefing meeting of the study.

In some cases, the sponsor of the research may express a desire to write the summary report. This desire may arise from an attempt to reduce the project budget or a belief that being more closely involved with the focus group topic allows the sponsor to bring better insights and experience to the reporting process. Even when the sponsor has taken copious notes and attended all of the groups, however, the research vendor should discourage the client from writing the report. Even good intentions run the risk of introducing bias into the study's results. If you are conducting a focus group study internally and are faced with writing the analysis yourself, be certain to seek one or two unbiased persons' opinions before you finalize your conclusions and recommendations.

Tools for Analysis

Several sources of information are useful tools for focus group analysis. These are listed in Table 5-1.

Table 5-1 Tools for Focus Group Analysis

The moderator's own notes taken during the groups

Notes taken by those viewing the focus groups

Debriefing sessions conducted immediately following each group

Audio- and/or videotapes of the focus groups

Focus group transcripts

Pregroup (or in-group) questionnaires

Moderator's Notes

Occasionally a moderator will take notes during the focus groups. Detailed notes are not really feasible, or the moderator's train of thought would be disrupted, as would the flow of the discussion. Rather, he or she should mark down only very important comments, not necessarily in the form of complete quotations.

These notes help by allowing the moderator to keep a record of specific segments of the conversation he or she wants to remember when reviewing the tapes. These notes provide the moderator with a record of his or her first impressions, which might otherwise be lost when viewing the videotapes. They remind him or her to look for that particular issue to consider in the reporting phase.

Viewers' Notes

Dependent on the nature of the groups, the moderator may have a research counterpart taking down notes in the viewing room. These notes allow for a more detailed series of areas to check on following the groups. Such notes should *not* be considered even partial transcripts of the focus groups, as there is substantial room for error. Notes generally consist more of general ideas discussed, rather than continuous direct quotations from group participants.

Clients viewing the groups may also provide the moderator with notes. These again should be considered only as an indicator of what to review more thoroughly. Client viewers are likely to insert their own opinions about or perceptions of the comments, thereby adding some bias to their notes.

Debriefing Sessions

Following each focus group, it is standard practice for the moderator/analyst to meet with the client and selected viewers to "debrief." During this ***debriefing session,*** they discuss relevant issues from the group, including surprising findings and areas that should be probed more heavily in the next groups. Some typical questions the moderator (or client) might ask during the debriefing could include the following:

- What did we learn here that is similar to prior groups in the study?

- What differed from the prior groups?

- Do we want to add any of the issues brought up in this session to the remaining groups?

The debriefing is *not* the place to begin analyzing the data. Too often clients (and sometimes overeager moderators) jump to conclusions following the first group or two in a study. The only time to seriously look for conclusions is after all of the groups have been completed.

It is important to note that both the viewers' notes and the debriefing sessions allow for direct input from the client. The moderator is responsible for sifting through such input to avoid biasing the results. It is acceptable, however, to take into consideration the client's expertise related to the topic. The client may be able to clarify certain technical aspects and provide some different perspectives on the participants' responses.

Audio- and/or Videotapes

The primary tool used in focus group reporting is the review of the audio- and/or videotapes from each of the focus groups. Depending again on the complexity of the subject matter, a full transcription of the tapes may be advisable to allow for a more accurate analysis.

The recordings allow the reporter to include pertinent quotations and to ensure that he or she correctly (and completely) heard the information discussed in the groups. In addition, nonverbal reactions (such as body language) can be reobserved on videotapes for inclusion in the report as applicable.

Focus Group Transcripts

Frequently, in addition to viewing the videotapes from the focus groups, the moderator will request that transcriptions be made from the tapes. These *focus group transcripts* do not provide all of the feedback from the respondents (body language cannot be expressed in this format), but they are still a useful tool. For example, seeing the exact quotations in print is helpful when trying to identify specific quotes for inclusion in the context of the report.

Pregroup (or In-Group) Questionnaires

As mentioned in Chapter 4, sometimes participants are asked to complete brief questionnaires (either before the groups or during the session itself). The results of such surveys are qualitative but can add depth to the moderator's understanding of the participants. If the moderator knows more about the participants' purchasing habits, job responsibilities, environmental attitudes, or any other issue that might pertain to the subject being discussed, then he or she can review the results of the study with this information in mind. Background about the participants may help to explain why they responded in a certain way during the group discussions.

Techniques in Focus Group Evaluation

The format of a focus group report varies by vendor styles and client preferences. Ultimately, however, all such reports aim to incorporate the overall essence of all of the focus group discussions included in a given qualitative project. To accomplish this, the writer may use a variety of techniques. Means of looking at and evaluating the focus group results can include the following:

- Grouping similar responses by quota group (for instance, mentions by region, age group, or company size)

- Identifying comments that are frequently mentioned

- Evaluating rankings or "votes" occurring over the course of the project

- Discussing messages with opposing ideas indicated by body language

To ensure accurate evaluation of focus group reports, keep in mind several rules of thumb:

- Avoid quantifying results; remember this is qualitative analysis.

- It is important to provide quotations to support your evaluations.

- Identify which thoughts were generated through a free-flowing discussion and which were actually aided responses.

- When reporting, it is often necessary to split or condense participants' quotations to more quickly make your point. This frequently occurs in the reports shown in Appendix C. For example, a participant says, "I really like the concept because it's something that I've never seen before; it's new and exciting like when they first introduced that microwavable oatmeal." The oatmeal doesn't pertain to the product being discussed, but the quote is good up to that point. Without losing the meaning of the quotation, the analyst might include the quote in the report as "I really like the concept because it's something that I've never seen before; it's new and exciting . . . ," or, shorter still: "I really like the concept . . . it's new and exciting." The key to remember is that you cannot change the meaning of the quotation, or the results of the study are likely to suffer.

Key Report Deliverables

While the content of the reporting process is typically best left to the discretion (and expertise) of the moderator, the "how" of the reporting process generally depends on the client's preferences. The final focus group project evaluation can consist of a number of building blocks, including these:

- An executive summary report (primarily the key findings and recommendations)

- A detailed report (generally containing detailed quotations and expanding on issues leading to the key findings)

- Focus group transcripts (including the actual video- and/or audiotapes)

- A presentation of results (potentially including tape excerpts as well)

Executive Summary Report

Dependent on your research vendor, the format and length of the executive summary report can vary greatly. Some researchers provide a summary that gives an overview of the study's objectives and the methodology, then simply lists the key findings and recommendations resulting from the groups. This may serve as the research presentation as well.

Other vendors flesh out the executive summary report, combining it with the more detailed evaluation of the results. This format typically includes direct quotations from the participants taken from the videotapes and transcriptions of the groups. In the sample reports included in Appendix C, the reporting style follows this format. Frequently, the reports follow the flow established in the discussion guide. You can see this by referring back to the discussion guides related to each of the sample reports. (These appear in Appendix B.)

The presentation of recommendations in focus group reports is a special case when clients want to make their own recommendations for actions to be taken based upon the focus group results. When this is the case, the executive summary may consist of a "key findings" or "conclusions" section and avoid listing formal recommendations. Vendors may also choose this approach out of cautiousness about the possible liabilities should a client follow the vendor's recommendation and suffer losses as a result. If you, as the client, expect the vendor to provide actionable recommendations as part of your research deliverables, you should clarify this during the proposal and contract phase.

A Detailed Report

As noted earlier, many vendors combine the detailed summary of the focus groups with the executive summary. This detailed report is generally where the participants' quotations are incorporated into the report. Key findings, expressed in brief format in the executive summary report, are expanded in the detailed report and explained in much greater depth. Although the executive summary is what management reads most often, the "meat" of your focus group analysis is in the detailed report.

Focus Group Transcripts

Frequently, the vendor will provide the client with the written transcripts of the focus groups. These are the verbatim scripts from each group as taken from the videotapes of the groups. While occasionally they provide interesting reading materials, it is often better not to spend as much time with these as with the report itself. It is far too easy to jump to one's own conclusions from the transcripts without considering the complete context in which comments were made or without taking into account other groups' reactions. The transcripts are best utilized by the person writing the focus group report. They serve as a reminder of where to look for specific quotes on the tapes, as well as ensuring that comments are properly quoted in the report.

Once the reporting is complete, the vendor usually provides the client with the videotapes of the groups. These tapes help to emphasize issues covered in the report, particularly for managers or other decision makers who might have been unable to attend the groups in person.

Presentation of Results

A focus group study presentation is unlike any quantitative study presentation you may have seen. The presenter cannot show colorful graphs and charts to illustrate his or her findings. More likely, the client will receive an executive summary report that answers the following questions:

- What was the purpose of the study?

- What were our research objectives?

- What methodology did we use, and why?

- Who did we talk with in the groups?

- What were our key findings?

- As a result, what do we recommend?

Pros and Cons of Doing It Yourself

In a "Walden-like" existence, a perfect world, the client will always have a research budget and will always commission a research vendor to do the study. This, of course, does not always happen. While it is not preferable to conduct focus groups internally, there can be some inherent advantages that outweigh the disadvantages in some cases.

Pros

Marketers may conduct their own focus groups because of at least two primary benefits: budgetary advantages and a superior knowledge base of the moderator.

Budgetary Advantages

Focus group research entails a wide range of expenses. By conducting its own focus groups utilizing internal resources, a company can either delete or, at the very least, substantially decrease many of these costs. The costs that will be most significantly decreased typically would include design (i.e., screener and discussion guide development), facility fees (if the company holds the groups on-site), focus group moderation, and analysis and reporting. The company may also lower the recruiting costs if it has an internal resource for this process.

Knowledge Base of Moderator

While a professional moderator is, without a doubt, much less biased about a company's study than anyone at the company, employees are more likely to have greater knowledge about the issues to be discussed in the focus groups. That understanding of the terminology, the market, and so forth can be valuable, provided the internal moderator can keep personal preferences regarding the outcome of the study from leading the group participants.

Cons

On the other hand, of course, there are obvious disadvantages to the marketer conducting focus groups. As with the benefits, this list could be longer, but we will concentrate on the two primary arguments against a company conducting its own focus groups: bias and the cost of poor research.

Bias

While an internal moderator may have extensive knowledge regarding the focus group subject matter, the flip side of the coin is that this knowledge may do more harm than good. However well intentioned, an internal moderator is likely to word questions in a manner that leads participants to support the moderator's views regarding the discussion topic. It is difficult not to put words in a participant's mouth, particularly if they are words related to a product you helped to develop!

The Cost of Poor Research

An untrained moderator (and, as noted, particularly a biased one) can unwittingly change the results of a study. By leading the participants or even by omitting pertinent questions or failing to clarify issues that arise during the groups, the moderator can prevent the true results from emerging from the discussion. Not only does this waste the money spent on the groups themselves, but worse still, if poor decisions are based on the research results, the company will incur greater costs.

It is tempting to conduct the research in-house to "save on the budget," but remember that you may be asking for problems. Whenever possible, the better solution is to look to an outside research vendor to conduct the study. The client can add valuable input throughout the study during the design phases.

Other Focus Group Situations

As the use of focus groups grows more widespread and sophisticated, the technique is being applied to a number of situations that pose special challenges. Among the most common of these situations are the following:

- International focus groups

- Focus groups with children or teens

- Focus groups with senior citizens

- Testing of prototypes/concepts prior to the focus group sessions

- Ad hoc problem-solving

This chapter introduces the issues to consider in each of these situations.

International Focus Groups

Technically, focus groups conducted abroad (defined here as outside of the United States) are designed and carried out in a similar manner to focus groups conducted domestically. The cost of international focus groups is significantly greater, however. In addition, a number of other potential differences deserve consideration during preparations to conduct international focus groups. Table 7-1 provides a checklist of these considerations.

Table 7-1 International Focus Group Issues

Sampling and recruiting requirements

Facilities: differences and distances

Language barriers

Cultural differences

Sampling and Recruiting Requirements

People in most other cultures, even those that Americans believe to be very similar (including Western European countries), tend to place a higher value on their personal privacy than do Americans. It therefore can be much more difficult to obtain accurate telephone or mailing lists when conducting an international study. Likewise, greater wariness on the part of contacts can substantially lower completion rates.

To help alleviate these problems, it is helpful to work with well-established research firms within each country you plan to conduct a study in. The best solution is to utilize the services of one firm experienced with international research to coordinate the subcontracting vendors. Be certain to have all materials such as screener questionnaires and discussion guides translated into the required languages. These materials should then be "back-translated" into English to ensure that the true intent of the wording is coming across properly in the translated versions. Poor translations lead possible recruits to doubt the profession-alism of the researchers and can potentially decrease your recruitment rates.

It is also advisable to check dates and times carefully when scheduling groups. Avoid setting up groups on local holidays, and be certain to schedule groups at times that circumvent the rush hours, mealtimes, and other activities of the local partici-pants. In Europe, for example, groups tend to start a bit later, such as 6:30 P.M. rather than the 5:30 or 6:00 P.M. timing often set in the United States.

Facilities: Differences and Distances

Do not expect that a focus group room in Singapore will be the same as a focus group room in Detroit. Not all foreign focus group facilities will boast a one-way mirror. In some cases, clients view groups via video monitors only. In others, you may find a very small mirror that will not comfortably accommodate more than two or three viewers.

The quality of video- and audiotaping may vary widely among the facilities you select internationally. In one instance, I encountered an arrangement where an ancient tape recorder was somehow wired to a video camera. The only sound recording was to be obtained through the tape recorder, while the video picked up only the visual portion of the groups. When the tape recorder somehow jammed, the only tape of my group was in effect a silent movie! Pregroup tests of the video and audio equipment are particularly important for international groups.

Also, clients do not always have access to food and beverages in the same manner we are accustomed to at home. While such amenities can, of course, be requested, often meal requests need to be made several days in advance; food deliveries are not common in many areas. Ice is not generally provided with beverages abroad as it is in the United States; if preferred, then arrangements should be made in advance.

It is also very important to ship any materials required for the focus groups to the facilities well in advance of the groups (at least two weeks ahead of time) to ensure receipt and clearance through customs. If possible, take an extra set of any crucial materials, prototypes, and so forth as part of your luggage to provide backup. This may seem a bit excessive, but it is better than getting caught without the required tools at the start of a group session.

Language Barriers

In addition to the translation issues discussed earlier, a number of other language-related issues need to be addressed with international focus groups. Moderators must be able to speak the required language(s) fluently. If your study is highly technical, you will also want to ensure that both the translator of the discussion guide and the moderator are using the correct terminology and in the correct context. Also, groups are often conducted in more than one country using several different moderators. In such cases, you will want to be sure that all of the moderators are briefed in the same manner. This is often best accomplished by a videoconference briefing (your moderators should also speak English) presided over by your primary vendor.

While the focus groups may be conducted in French, German, and Chinese, it is important that the viewers understand the discussion. The best solution to meet this concern is a simultaneous interpretation process. An interpreter sits either in a small sound booth off of the focus group room or in the viewing room with the clients. He or she then repeats in English (for American businesspeople) what is said in the discussion. Granted, this is not always a perfect situation. I have endured interpreters who ate while talking and who tried to insert every cough or laugh from the conversation into their interpreted version. All things considered, however, the process generally works quite well. What is slightly disconcerting is getting adjusted to hearing one voice throughout the groups instead of eight different voices making their comments.

The videotapes of the focus groups will need to be dubbed over in English as well. Typically, the interpreter's version of the discussion will be overlaid on the video. While it will not match the video very well, it will still be viewable. You can also have direct translations done and then overlaid on the video; these will match better but will prove significantly more expensive. For reporting purposes, however, it is advisable to have the groups' actual verbiage (versus the interpreter's version) translated and transcribed. This will provide verbatim comments, which may have been reworded and occasionally missed in the simultaneous interpretation process.

A final issue regarding language barriers with international groups is the language of any materials to be tested in the groups. Double-check your translations on any visual materials (storyboards, packaging, videos, etc.), audiotapes (of radio advertisements, etc.), or products (software, etc.) that will be tested in the groups. Likewise, any cost figures to be discussed should be converted into the local currency.

Cultural Differences

One cannot go to another country and assume that the same rules apply. The old adage "when in Rome . . ." definitely applies well to focus group research abroad. For example, as noted earlier, in many countries confidentiality and privacy are much more crucial issues for participants. Only first names can be provided to clients in the participant profile matrices, and in many cases, participants will disclose the *type* of company they work for, but not the name of the company. This concern for participant privacy is one explanation for why foreign focus group facilities do not always provide one-way mirrors for viewing; they are considered too intrusive. In some instances, clients are not even allowed to receive the videotapes from the groups, although the vendor may use them for reporting purposes.

The overall atmosphere in international focus groups can also differ substantially from the American norm. While in the United States smoking in the focus group facility would be considered inappropriate, in Europe, for example, even the participants (and occasionally the moderators) smoke during the groups. Often in the United States, clients are served wine or beer in the client viewing room, but in Europe the alcoholic beverages can be served to the participants as well.

You should also be conscious of socially acceptable mixes of participants. For example, does the country in which you plan to conduct groups generally accept men and women meeting in groups together outside of the typical work environment? Would a female moderator be viewed as inappropriate by a focus group consisting of entirely male participants? Do not make assumptions when planning international focus groups; check out all of the details in order to avoid difficulties later.

Focus Groups with Children or Teens

Frequently, particularly within specific industries, the target markets from which focus groups must be pulled together are young children or teens. Such groups could, for example, be focusing on testing new toy concepts, evaluating educational software products, or identifying attitudes related to fashion trends. Focus groups with younger participants are coordinated in a manner similar to those arranged for adult participants. There are, however, several nuances you should carefully consider when designing, recruiting, and conducting these groups.

First, the recommended methodology with younger participants is the in-person focus group. Telefocus groups may not permit the moderator to maintain the necessary control in the groups, and you also risk losing participants' attention. In addition, such groups may not allow younger participants to feel as comfortable with the research situation, so they may provide less input regarding the topic.

While other moderators may offer varying opinions, I recommend mini groups (five or six participants) with younger children and mini or full-sized focus groups (eight to ten participants) with teens. These groups allow interaction while not requiring each individual participant to *constantly* speak (as would be the case, for instance, with triads). This creates a greater comfort level and is, therefore, more conducive to a successful discussion.

Recruiting Minors

The process of recruiting minors for focus groups must include their parents or legal guardians. When calling, either via random-digit dialing or from a purchased list of names, interviewers should first ask to speak with the minor's parent or guardian. The initial part of the screening process would provide the parent with general information regarding why the study is being conducted and how the focus group process works. The interviewer would ask the adult questions related to the child's demographics (age, grade level, etc.) and potentially clarification issues related to the focus group subject matter (e.g., "Does your child have access to a personal computer at home?" or "What brand(s) of jeans does your child wear?"). The parent *must* agree to allow his or her child to continue the screening with you and must also agree to arrange to get the child to the scheduled focus group.

When asking any additional screening questions to the child on the telephone, keep the questions simple and straightforward. Do not ask more than five questions, and keep the tone very friendly; you do not want to make children nervous about sharing their opinions in a group situation. Recruiting interviewers should be particularly aware of the child's tone during the screening process: Does the child seem overly shy or extremely outspoken? Is the child polite in his or her response or rather eager to get off the phone? Recruiters should note general perceptions regarding the child's potential ability to participate and add value to the focus group discussion.

Do *not* mention co-op fees to younger children unless they have expressed a genuine interest in the group for the sake of participating. If possible, do not tell them about the fees at all, but rather address that issue with their parents, then mention fees at the group, almost as a bonus rather than an incentive. Typically for focus groups conducted with minors, both parents and children receive a co-op fee for participation, since you must rely on the parents to get the children to the groups on time.

Confidentiality of participants' responses and personal information will also be of even greater concern when dealing with young participants. Parents generally want assurance that their children's identities will not be released outside of the focus group itself. Of particular concern will be the need to reassure parents that neither they nor their children will be inundated with sales efforts following the groups. (For more on ethics and focus group research, see Chapter 8.)

Scheduling and Preparing for the Groups

Scheduling focus groups for children can also take on a different dimension than for those conducted with adults. It is prudent to avoid groups during certain school vacation periods and close to major holidays. Even if you do manage to recruit participants, your no-show rate is likely to increase during these times. Likewise, check local calendars to avoid coinciding with regional events that could further prevent good focus group attendance.

How a focus group room is arranged can also play a part in the success (or likewise the failure) of a focus group with children. Even though viewers may not see all reactions as clearly, it is better not to have the children look directly toward the one-way mirror.

This can cause quite a distraction when they start making funny faces at their reflections. Also, conference room chairs that spin or have wheels can cause a lot of unexpected motion in the groups and slow the discussion process.

Refreshments should be provided at the facility for both the adults and the children involved in the group process. Give children their refreshments before the discussion, as it can be disruptive during the groups. At one facility where I conducted groups with eight-, nine-, and ten-year-olds, the hostess brought pizza into the room just as we were getting started. We lost ten minutes of valuable discussion time while the children got settled with their food. In addition, the grease was not exactly conducive to testing the client's new writing utensils! Even the simplest aspects of the focus groups need to be carefully considered when the groups involve a younger audience.

Conducting Focus Groups with Children

In terms of the actual focus group session with children, keep the groups somewhat shorter than the ninety-minute groups typically conducted with adult participants. Sixty to seventy-five minutes is preferable, as it allows less time for attention levels to decrease. It is also important to avoid trying to cover too many issues in a children's focus group; it can confuse the children and therefore the results as well. The moderator should, whenever possible, incorporate activities that keep the children's attention focused and keep them interested in the subject being covered.

Group conformities can also arise in children's groups, more so than in adult groups. In other words, participants will agree with others in the group to avoid standing out. The moderator can help stem this by frequently asking if anyone has "other ideas" or "different opinions."

Certain types of questions are particularly ineffective in children's groups and should, therefore, be avoided. These would include questions such as the following:

- *"Which of these products would you be most likely to purchase?"* Children (at least younger ones) are not likely to evaluate concepts in terms of trade-offs. They want one, the other, or both for their own individual attributes, not necessarily because one is better than the other, less expensive, or more durable. Questions need to be asked in terms that relate to the participants involved. For example, it would be better to ask, "Billy, what do you like about product X?" then, "Billy, what do you like about product Y?" and alternately identify Billy's dislikes about the same products. Did he like more aspects of one product than the other? Overall, what *appeared* to be trade-offs within the group? It becomes more of a reporting issue, whereas you could ask adults which is better for them and why.

- *"How much would you be willing to pay for product X?"*
  Children are likely to have a difficult time relating an appropriate price to a given product concept. To a child, what may seem a large dollar figure may actually be underpriced for the product being studied. Such information would likely prove unreliable and, in many cases, irrelevant, since parents are typically the actual purchasers acting on input from their children.

- *"Last year, what was your favorite action figure?"*
  Younger children do not necessarily remember things that happened in the past as precisely as an adult might. Asking about last week may be pushing your luck, let alone trying to dredge up actions from several months to a year ago. Questions are better worded in the present: "Sam, what action figures do you have at home?" "Which one(s) do you play with a lot?"

- *"Next Christmas, what toys will you ask your mom and dad for?"*
  This is similar to the preceding point regarding questions about past actions. Children will not necessarily like the same toys two months from the time the group is conducted. Fads come and go, and interests change rapidly. Today's toy is quickly cast aside for another, newer option. It is better to look at, for example, qualities that they consistently seem interested in, rather than specific toys or brands. Also, never assume that they will do what they say they will even one day down the road. And don't assume the participants celebrate this holiday—refer to occasions like birthdays that don't risk introducing cultural bias. (This is much the same as it is for adults.)

Often children's groups can be more successful from an observational standpoint, particularly with younger children. For example, doing away with the formal "conference room" atmosphere and simply watching children interact, do role-playing exercises, or play with a selection of toys may be more productive than a structured discussion on a specific topic.

Focus Groups with Senior Citizens

As with conducting international or children's focus groups, conducting focus groups with senior citizens, particularly those seventy years of age and over, requires some additional planning. This section looks at major issues (both from logistics and from moderating standpoints) that should be considered when planning focus groups with senior citizens.

Many senior citizens no longer drive or are without their own transportation. Participants may need to hitch a ride to get to the scheduled group. Be prepared to accommodate spouses or friends in a waiting area, and provide refreshments and reading materials for them. Also, be sure in your planning stages to strongly consider facilities that are located on public transportation routes. In addition, while there is a tendency to assume that lower co-op payments would still draw participants from older age groups, consider that they may need to pay for public transportation or cabs in order to attend, so co-op fees should be somewhat higher than might initially be assumed.

Seniors tend to be cautious about attending groups, particularly if the facility is in an unfamiliar neighborhood or downtown area. When planning focus groups specifically targeting senior citizens, select facilities that have well-marked, illuminated entrances and are easily entered from a main street. Facilities should also be accessible for wheelchairs and walkers. Do not expect your participants to enter from a side door off an alley and climb two flights of stairs! During the recruiting process, provide general directions to the facility and strongly reassure them that they will receive a detailed map and directions (in large print).

As seniors are frequently targeted in fraudulent schemes, they are often more skeptical during the recruiting process and therefore more difficult to recruit. Whenever possible in the recruiting process, avoid asking income-related or other extremely personal questions. Also, if it does not hurt the integrity of the research study, it is usually helpful to identify the sponsor of the study to legitimize it in the eyes of the recruits.

Many seniors now continue working well past what was once considered the age of retirement. Researchers can no longer assume this target market can readily attend daytime focus groups. While many seniors, of course, do retire, many choose to continue working or must continue working to maintain an adequate income to live on. Do not assume that daytime groups will cover this target market; it is likely that you will still need to conduct groups in the evening. Seniors are less likely to hear and see as clearly as participants in your other targeted age groups. When preparing concept materials or advertising tapes/videos, be conscious of these potential issues in senior groups. Items to be read should be available in slightly larger print or written clearly and somewhat larger than you might normally write on a flip chart or whiteboard. Be considerate when playing tapes of any type for the group by ensuring that the sound is at a level that all group participants can clearly distinguish.

Testing Prototypes/Concepts Prior to Focus Groups

Some research topics are better covered once the focus group participants have had a more detailed hands-on experience than the typical ninety-minute discussion session allows. Researchers struggle with these situations, because they can lead to problems in terms of confidentiality. For example, assume that a start-up software company wants to test its new business graphics package. The product is expected to allow the company to compete head on with "the big guys," and the developers want feedback from potential users to ensure that they are meeting their goal of being user-friendly yet high-powered. The research vendor can, of course, conduct all testing in a focus group environment; either via exercises on boards and screens or combined with hands-on use of computers during the groups. To get feedback based on real-life situations, however, it might be preferable to allow recruits to test the program in their own work environments.

One possible solution is to recruit participants, ensure that they will be able to attend the scheduled groups, and then fax nondisclosure agreements to them. Once participants return these signed forms, sample disks or CDs would be sent to them to test. It is advisable that such samples not include a product or company name, to further guarantee confidentiality for the client. Once the test period is completed, participants would be required to bring the disks with them to the groups in order to receive their co-op fee.

Another suggested option for prototype or concept testing in advance of the discussion groups is the use of an Internet survey. Recruits could be invited to visit a secured Web site prior to participating in a focus group. There, upon giving a preassigned password, they could, for example, view certain aspects of the product and respond to various questions to be later expanded upon in the group sessions.

While these suggested methodologies do emphasize confidentiality, there is no guaranteed method of avoiding corporate espionage, particularly when you send concept diagrams or product prototypes into business environments. Be aware of the potential issues, and weigh the research needs in comparison to the possible problems before rushing in.

In addition, remember that any type of pregroup survey still results in *qualitative* information. You can learn added information about participants and their opinions through pregroup surveys, but do not make the mistake of assuming that the data are quantifiable.

Ad Hoc Problem Solving

Seldom is a focus group study conducted without at least one or two mishaps occurring during the initial process or, more difficult still, the night of the groups. Following are just a few of the possible problems that can (and do) occur:

- Too few participants show up for a group.

- Recruiting runs too slowly and will not be finished in time to meet the focus group schedule.

- Participants bring the kids along (or, worse still, an outspoken spouse!).

- One participant is particularly arrogant and disruptive.

- The recording equipment fails on the night of the groups.

- Your moderator is unable to conduct a group due to an emergency.

- The prototypes you shipped in advance do not arrive in time for the groups.

The list, no doubt, could go on and on, with each research vendor and client adding his or her own "favorite" focus group horror stories. What is key to the success of your focus group research, however, is to be able to know what can be salvaged while maintaining the integrity of the study and when it is simply better to reassess your schedule and postpone the groups.

Let's consider some possible solutions to each of the previously mentioned problems.

Too Few Participants

When too few participants show up, the best solution depends somewhat on the time line for your project and how many similar groups you have already conducted. If you have done several groups consisting of participants with similar qualifications, you could either cancel the group altogether or simply conduct the group as a mini group (or as a triad if attendance is extremely bad!).

If this is the first group, time permits, and there is a definite issue with the quality of the recruiting that was done, you might ask the vendor to replace this particular group (preferably at a reduced rate or no additional charge). If the poor show rate is due to factors beyond the vendor's control, then you may want to choose to conduct a mini group to avoid further losses in terms of time and funds. Use it, for example, as an initial test of the discussion guide. While you will probably still want to replace (or augment) this group with another, similar one, a small group session could still serve a purpose.

Recruiting Behind Schedule

When recruiting falls behind schedule, your best bet again may be to extend the recruitment period and postpone the groups slightly. It is better to have good groups than quick groups! Still, reevaluate what specifically may be affecting the recruiting time. Did the vendor miscalculate the number of interviewers to assign to recruiting for the project, or did they begin recruiting too late? Or is it difficult to meet strict quotas, or do they have poor lists? Determine what you can do to move the process along at a more acceptable rate.

Participants Accompanied by Family Members

As noted in Chapter 2, sometimes focus group participants may ask if they can bring along their children, spouse, or friends to their assigned group. If they ask, the problem can be circumvented. But what if they simply bring others along without asking permission first? Under no circumstances should these additional people be invited to join the group; they were not recruited and are not likely to fit the required profile.

For the adults, you basically have two options: you can allow them to remain in the waiting room, or you can ask them to leave the facility. Remember that if you ask them to leave, you are likely to have to release the participant as well. If the extra people are children, it is best to send them home, as it is unreasonable to expect the host(ess) to play the role of baby-sitter as well. In these instances, you will definitely be sending the related participant home, too.

Under these circumstances, it is acceptable to withhold the co-op fee, as the participant did not arrive at the facility with the intent to participate as agreed. Rather, he or she expected a friend or spouse to join in as well or the facility to provide child care.

Arrogant and Disruptive Participant

In instances where one participant is rude to the moderator and/or the other focus group participants, it is always preferable to release the participant from the group. Whether you choose to pay him or her the co-op fee probably depends upon the level of abuse occurring in the group.

While disagreements are expected during the course of the discussion, participants are expected to present their differing opinions in a manner respectful of the others in the group. When one participant is loud and argumentative and prevents others from freely expressing opposing ideas, then that participant is likely to affect the quality of the research results. Other participants may be afraid to join in because they do not want to deal with the abusive personality.

Recording Equipment Failure

If you arrive at the groups an hour or so prior to the first session, you should be able to have the vendor test the video and audio recording equipment. If it is not working well at this point, you can usually remedy the situation by switching rooms (many facilities have more than one focus group room) if another is available or by having the vendor arrange for a professional videotaping service to come in.

If it is too late to make such arrangements, you may have to rely on videotaping only or audiotaping only (it is unlikely that both will have failed unless there is a problem with circuits or the microphone). While this option is not preferable, it is better than releasing and paying for all participants in groups on that date. If videotaping is crucial to your project (as with concept testing and hands-on exercises), you should suggest to the vendor that, unless suitable taping is available for the scheduled groups, they should replace the group(s) that will not be taped due to the equipment problems. The videotaping is the vendor's responsibility and should be in working condition to meet your needs.

Moderator Unavailable

Only rarely does an emergency make a professional moderator unavailable, but a good case of laryngitis can throw a wrench in the best-planned focus groups. Typically, vendors have backup moderators who can be brought up to speed quickly and take over the study. Even consultants who operate on their own generally know of other moderators they could call on to step in due to an emergency. If you are comfortable with the last-minute change, then the groups can go on as scheduled. If, however, the groups are highly technical or you are less than comfortable with the moderator who is replacing your contracted vendor, it is advisable to postpone the groups if at all possible.

If you as a client are uncomfortable with the vendor or do not believe he or she is familiar enough with the subject matter, then it will be hard to accept the findings of the study. You (and/or your colleagues) may then question whether the findings would have been different if the original moderator (who was up to speed with the project) had been available.

No Prototypes on Hand

If you shipped prototypes to the facility but they did not arrive in time, the complexity of the prototypes will be your deciding factor on what to do. If the groups are supposed to involve a great deal of hands-on testing with the prototypes, then you must postpone the groups and reschedule the participants if possible. Participants who cannot be reached prior to showing up for the groups should be compensated with their promised co-op fee. This will give you a better chance of getting them to attend a rescheduled session.

If, however, these are your initial groups and the prototypes are easily described or sketched out on a flip chart (obviously not the best option, but potentially workable), you may consider testing the discussion guide in the scheduled groups. You will already have paid for the moderator, the facility, and the participants, so why not test the general ideas as much as possible?

Finally, whose responsibility were the shipments? If the vendor was responsible for the shipments, did he or she allow adequate time for them to reach the facility? If not, and the problem is definitely the fault of the vendor, the client can ask for the groups to be replaced. If the error is the client's, the client will be expected to pay the costs associated with replacing the groups.

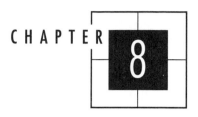

CHAPTER 8

Ethics in Focus Group Research

In any business situation, it is expected that all parties involved will perform their roles in an ethical manner. This is equally true with focus group research. Each person involved in the focus group study, whether client, vendor, or participant, should be able to expect certain standards to be met. While this chapter is brief, do not underestimate the importance of these expectations. Following are some issues that each of the players in a focus group study has the right to expect.

Expectations of the Client

The client should . . .

- receive fair pricing from the vendor.

- expect total confidentiality from the vendor. The design, discussions, and results will not be released without the client's permission.

- receive *honest* recruiting. The vendor will not ask a nephew or next-door neighbor to participate in order to fill a group quickly.

- expect unbiased moderating and reporting from the vendor.

Expectations of the Vendor

The vendor should . . .

- be invited to bid on equal footing with other vendors. Other vendors should not be asked to bid if a favored vendor is guaranteed to win the project.

- have estimated pricing accepted rather than being expected to lower prices to gain a given or future project.

- be able to analyze focus group outcomes without the client dictating what results must be provided. (The format can be specified, but not the results!)

- collect all diagrams, notes, and materials from participants at the end of each focus group session to ensure confidentiality for the client.

Expectations of Participants

The participant should . . .

- have the right to refuse the invitation to attend a group without being harassed by recruiters who need to meet a quota.

- be informed of all video- and audiotaping occurring during the groups, as well as advised that people are viewing the groups.

- feel comfortable within the group setting. No participant should be forced to respond, expected to answer in a given manner, or humiliated for having differing opinions.

- be able to rely on the safety of the facility and its parking lot area.

- receive an honest explanation about how the research results will be used.

- not be put into a situation that is actually a sales presentation when he or she is expecting to attend a discussion group. (There is a difference!)

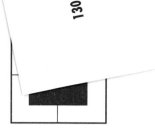

Glossary

Blind study   A study in which participants are not told who the research client or sponsor is

Clarification   The process of asking participants to further define their responses—for example, to identify what a technical term means

Co-moderator   A second moderator working in conjunction with the moderator, typically to assist with demonstrations and the discussion

Confirmation call   A follow-up call to a focus group recruit, typically one day prior to the group in order to ensure that the recruit will attend

Confirmation letter   A letter sent to someone recruited for a focus group to acknowledge that the person has agreed to participate, to remind him or her of the date and time of the group, and to provide him or her with directions to the focus group facility

Co-op fee   A payment made to a focus group participant, usually in the form of cash, also called cooperation fee or incentive

Debriefing session   A meeting between the moderator and the research study client that follows a focus group (or series of focus groups) to discuss initial findings and fine-tune the discussion guide used for future focus groups

Discussion guide   An outline used by a focus group moderator to assist in conducting the discussion in an orderly manner and to ensure that all necessary topics are covered during the group

Dyad   A qualitative research discussion conducted with only two participants

Executive summary report   A brief report summarizing the research objectives of a study, the methodology, the key findings, and the resulting recommendations

Focus group   A research discussion group conducted by a moderator and designed to create a free-flowing conversation about one or more issues related to a general topic

Focus group transcript   Verbatim scripts of the focus group sessions taken from the videotapes

Host(ess)   Person appointed at the vendor's facility to set up the groups, handle refreshments for participants and clients, ensure that the groups are taped, and assist in communications between the moderator and clients during the group sessions

Industry-sensitive questions   Questions asked during the screening interview to exclude competitors or industry experts from the groups, so as to avoid biasing the study or breaching confidentiality

Internet focus group   A focus group recruited and conducted on-line via the Internet

Mini focus group   A focus group consisting of five or six participants

Moderator   A focus group facilitator whose main role is to keep the discussion on track and elicit comments related to meeting the study's research objectives

One-on-one interview   A less structured "survey" or discussion conducted in person by an interviewer with one participant at a time

Participant profile matrix   A chart that identifies recruits' responses to key screening questions

Probing   The process by which a moderator encourages focus group participants to elaborate on their responses

Qualitative research   A relatively unstructured research method such as focus groups where the results are open to subjective interpretation

Quantitative research   A structured research method designed to provide statistically valid results in the form of numbers and percentages

Quota group   A preassigned segment of the sample to be recruited for a specific focus group or groups

Recruiter   Telephone interviewer who conducts screening interviews to identify and schedule qualified focus group participants

Recruiting   The process of contacting, qualifying, and scheduling potential focus group participants

Recruiting profile   A predetermined definition of participants needed in each focus group in order to meet the research objectives

Research objectives   Specifications of what the research team wants to learn from a research study

Sample   List of contact names used to recruit focus group participants

Screener questionnaire   A brief questionnaire that asks a series of questions designed to evaluate a contact's eligibility to participate in a specific focus group

Secondary information   Research and data already available for review, such as census information

Stand-alone video   A video camera set in one position to record a focus group discussion; typically wall-mounted in the focus group facility

Target market   A segment of the market or a group of potential customers to which a marketer directs an ad campaign, program, promotion, or product

Telefocus group   A focus group discussion conducted using a conference call

Triad   A qualitative discussion conducted with a group of three people

Video focus group   An in-person focus group discussion that clients view via videoconferencing

Viewing room   A small room outside the focus group room where clients can observe the focus group in progress via a one-way mirror and intercom

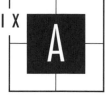

Sample Focus Group Screener Questionnaires

The five samples in this appendix are typical of focus group screener questionnaires. In each questionnaire, the numbered phrases in **bold type** identify important items to include. These items are defined as follows:

1. **Identification of the research vendor**—legitimizes the study

2. **General purpose of the study**—explains what participants can expect

3. **Confirmation that the call is not a sales call**—helps maintain cooperation

4. **Promise of confidentiality**—helps ensure honesty

5. **Industry-sensitive questions**—prevents biasing the study and protects the client

6. **Question(s) about recent focus group participation**—screen out "professional" participants

7. **Invitation to participate**—identifies the study as focus group research

8. **Co-op fee designation**—entices the candidate to follow through and attend the group

To learn principles of developing a screener questionnaire, see Chapter 2.

Community Recycling Study
Focus Group Screener

Date: ____/____/____

Call Start: __ __:__ __   **Call End:** __ __:__ __

Interviewer ID#: __ __ __ __

Phone: (__ __ __ **)** __ __ __ - __ __ __ __

[Ask to speak with head of household.]

Hello, my name is _____ with **(1) ABC Research**, an independent, local marketing research firm. We are conducting a **(2) study concerning recycling for Riverside City** and would appreciate your opinions. We are **(3) not selling anything** and will only take a few minutes of your time. **(4) All of your responses will be kept confidential.**

S1. First, are you 18 years of age or older and responsible for paying the garbage bill for your household?

> 1. Yes [continue to **S2**]
>
> 2. No [ask to speak to a qualified person; if not available thank and terminate]
>
> 3. Refused [thank and terminate]

S2. (5) Are you, or is anyone in your household, employed by an advertising agency or recycling facility?

1. Yes [thank and terminate]

2. No [continue to **S3**]

3. Don't know/refused [thank and terminate]

S3. (6) Have you ever participated in a focus group discussion for marketing research purposes for which you were paid for your time?

1. Yes [continue to **S4**]

2. No [skip to **S5**]

S4. (6) When was the last time you participated in a focus group discussion?

1. Less than 6 months ago [thank and terminate]

2. 6 months or more [continue to **S5**]

S5. Do you live within the Riverside City limits?

1. Yes [continue to **S6**]

2. No [thank and terminate]

3. Refused [thank and terminate]

S6. What is your zip code?

_____ [check quotas and continue to **S7**]

S7. Do you currently use recycling services that pick up recyclables where you live?

1. Yes

2. No

3. Don't know

4. Refused

S8. Which of the following best describes the home you live in? Is it . . . ? [Read list and record one only. Check quotas.]

1. Single-family home

2. Duplex

3. Triplex or fourplex

4. Condominium or townhouse

5. Apartment building or complex with more than 5 units

6. Mobile home

7. [Don't read] Refused [thank and terminate]

S9. I need to ask just a few questions for the purposes of classification for this study. First, which of the following categories best describes your age? [Read list and record one only. Check quotas.]

1. 18 to 34

2. 25 to 34

3. 35 to 44

4. 45 to 54

5. 55 to 64

6. Over 64

7. [Don't read] Refused [thank and terminate]

S10. What is the highest level of education you have had the opportunity to complete? [Don't read list. Record one only. Check quotas.]

1. Grade school

2. High school

3. Community college (2-year degree)

4. Vocational/technical college

5. Some college

6. College (4-year degree)

7. Some graduate studies

8. Graduate school (received degree)

9. Refused [thank and terminate]

S11. Which of the following best describes your ethnic background? [Read list and record one only. If needed, note that this is asked for statistical purposes only.]

1. African-American

2. Asian [Specify below:]

3. Vietnamese

4. Cambodian

5. Filipino

6. Japanese

7. Korean

8. Chinese

9. Other [Specify: _____]

10. Hispanic

11. Native American/American Indian

12. Caucasian

13. Other [Specify: _____]

14. [Don't read] Refused [thank and terminate]

S12. Which of the following *best* describes you? [Read list and record one only.]

1. I am too busy to pay much attention to recycling and things like that. [Check quota—50% in 6 P.M.; if not filled, continue to **S13**; if filled, skip to **S14**.]

2. I usually use a reusable coffee mug when I get coffee, and I reuse my grocery bags at the store or take a cloth bag. [Skip to **S14**.]

3. I pay attention to reducing, reusing, and recycling waste when I have time. [Check quota—50% in 6 P.M.; if not filled, continue to **S13**; if filled, skip to **S14**.]

4. [Don't read] Don't know [probe for best fit]

5. [Don't read] Refused [thank and terminate]

S13. As part of our research, **(7) we are inviting a group of people like yourself to participate in a discussion group.** There will be no attempt to sell you any product or service. These discussion groups are held for opinion purposes only. The group will be relaxed and informal, and you will simply be involved in an exchange of ideas and opinions.

The group will be held on Wednesday, September 14, at 6:00 P.M. It will last approximately 90 minutes, and because we value your time and opinions, **(8) we are offering a $35 cash honorarium** to those who participate. Will you be able to join us?

> 1. Yes [skip to information]
>
> 2. No [thank and terminate]
>
> 3. Don't know [arrange callback]

S14. As part of our research, **(7) we are inviting a group of people like yourself to participate in a discussion group.** There will be no attempt to sell you any product or service. These discussion groups are held for opinion purposes only. The group will be relaxed and informal, and you will simply be involved in an exchange of ideas and opinions.

The group will be held on Wednesday, September 14, at 8:00 P.M. It will last approximately 90 minutes, and because we value your time and opinions, **(8) we are offering a $35 cash honorarium to those who participate.** Will you be able to join us?

> 1. Yes [skip to information]

2. No [thank and terminate]

3. Don't know [arrange callback]

Information:

[Provide respondent with general location of facility if necessary. Explain that detailed directions will be sent soon.]

So that we can send you a confirmation letter and directions to the group, I need your full name and mailing address: [Probe for complete information.]

Name: _____

Address: _____

City/State: _____ Zip: _____

Also, I would like to confirm that the phone number I reached you at is:

[Read number from sample and record or correct it below.]

(_ _ _)_ _ _-_ _ _ _

Thank you for your time! We look forward to seeing you on Wednesday, September 14, at [time selected above].

Interviewer:

Record Gender: 1. Female 2. Male

Water Quality Study
Focus Group Screener

Date: __ __/__ __/__ __

Call Start: __ __:__ __ **Call End:** __ __:__ __

Interviewer ID#: __ __ __ __

Phone: (__ __ __)__ __ __-__ __ __ __

[Ask to speak with head of household.]

Hello, my name is _____ with the **(1)
Qualitative Research Specialists,** an independent market
research firm. We are conducting **(2) a study of area residents
concerning water quality** and would appreciate your input.
We are **(3)** *not* **selling anything** and will only take a few
minutes of your time. **(4) All of your responses will be kept
confidential.**

S1. First, are you between the ages of 25 and 54?

>   1. Yes [continue to **S2**]

>   2. No [thank respondent and terminate]

>   3. Refused [thank respondent and terminate]

**S2. (5) Are you or is anyone in your immediate household
employed by or otherwise directly affiliated with an
advertising agency or environmental firm or marketing
research company?**

1. Yes [thank respondent and terminate]

2. No [continue to **S3**]

3. Refused [thank respondent and terminate]

S3. (6) Have you participated in a focus group study within the past 6 months?

1. Yes [thank respondent and terminate]

2. No [continue to **S4**]

3. Don't know [thank respondent and terminate]

S4. Do you currently own or rent your residence?

1. Own [check quotas before continuing; if full, thank and terminate]

2. Rent [check quotas before continuing; if full, thank and terminate]

3. Refused [thank respondent and terminate]

S5. Which county do you live in?

1. Brown [check quotas; if full, thank and terminate]

2. Connor [check quotas; if full, thank and terminate]

3. Green [check quotas; if full, thank and terminate]

4. Other [thank respondent and terminate]

S6. Focus group discussions with area residents such as yourself are being conducted this month. The discussions will center on your perceptions of water quality in our region. The purpose of the groups is solely to obtain your opinions; no sales will be involved. The sessions will last approximately 90 minutes, and light refreshments will be served. In addition, **(8) you will receive $40 for your participation. (7) Would you be interested in attending one of these groups?**

1. Yes [continue to **S7**]

2. No [thank respondent and terminate]

3. Don't know [continue to **S7**]

4. Refused [thank respondent and terminate]

S7. The groups are scheduled for [Check quotas for availability] 6:00 P.M. and 8:00 P.M. on Wednesday, June 20, at Qualitative Research Specialists' facility in Anytown. Which group will you be able to attend?

1. 6 P.M. [continue to information section]

2. 8 P.M. [continue to information section]

3. Neither [thank respondent and terminate]

4. Don't know [schedule callback]

Participant Information:

[Provide respondent with general location of facility if necessary. Explain that detailed directions will be sent soon by mail.]

So that we can send you a confirmation letter and directions to the group, I need your full name and mailing address: [Probe for complete information.]

Name: _____

Address: _____

City/State: _____ Zip: _____

Also, I would like to confirm that the phone number that I reached you at is: [Read number from sample and record or correct it below.]

(_ _ _)_ _ _-_ _ _ _

Thank you for your time! We look forward to seeing you on June 20, at [time selected above].

Interviewer:

Record Gender: 1. Female 2. Male

Credit Union Senior Program Study
Focus Group Screener

Date: __ __/__ __/__ __

Call Start: __ __:__ __ **Call End:** __ __:__ __

Interviewer ID#: __ __ __ __

Phone: (__ __ __)__ __ __-__ __ __ __

[Ask to speak with person listed. If not available, arrange callback.]

Hello, my name is _____ with **(1) Focus Scope Research, calling on behalf of Acme Credit Union.** We are conducting a study among credit union members such as yourself and would appreciate your input **(2) concerning the credit union's products and your financial needs. (3) We are *not* selling anything** and will only take a few minutes of your time. **(4) All of your responses will be kept confidential,** and we will not ask you for any specific account information.

S1. First, are you the person in your household who conducts or shares equally in conducting your household's banking business?

> 1. Yes [continue to **S2**]
>
> 2. No [thank and terminate]
>
> 3. Don't know [thank and terminate]
>
> 4. Refused [thank and terminate]

S2. And are you 55 years of age or older?

    1. Yes [continue to **S3**]

    2. No [thank and terminate]

    3. Refused [thank and terminate]

S3. (5) Do you or does anyone in your household currently work for or serve on the board of any financial institution or work for a marketing research or advertising firm?

    1. Yes [thank and terminate]

    2. No [continue to **S4**]

    3. Don't know/refused [thank and terminate]

S4. (6) Have you participated in a financial services focus group within the past 6 months?

    1. Yes [thank and terminate]

    2. No [continue to **S5**]

    3. Don't know/refused [clarify, re-ask; otherwise thank and terminate]

S5. Focus Scope Research will be conducting focus group discussions with Acme Credit Union members such as yourself. The discussions will center on the credit union's product line and your own financial needs. The purpose of the groups is solely to obtain your opinions; *no* sales will be involved. The sessions will last approximately 90 minutes, and light refreshments will be served. In addition, **(8) you will**

receive $30 for your participation. (7) Would you be interested in attending a group?

> 1. Yes [continue to **S6**]
>
> 2. No [thank and terminate]
>
> 3. Don't know [if interested, go to **S6**; otherwise thank and terminate]
>
> 4. Refused [thank and terminate]

S6. [When 12 are recruited for one group, recruit only for the open group. Do not accept over 12 for either group.] The groups are scheduled for 4 P.M. and 6 P.M. on Thursday, July 16. Will you be able to attend either of these groups?

> 1. Yes [continue to information section]
>
> 2. No [thank and terminate]
>
> 3. Don't know [schedule callback]
>
> 4. Refused [thank and terminate]

Participant Information:

[Provide respondent with general location of facility. Explain that detailed directions will be sent by mail soon.]

Note group attending and exact age:

> 1. 4:00 P.M. Age: __ __
>
> 2. 6:00 P.M. Age: __ __

So that we can send you a confirmation letter and directions to the group, I need your full name and mailing address: [Probe for complete information.]

Name: _____

Address: _____

City/State: _____ Zip: _____

Also, I would like to confirm that the phone number I reached you at is: [Read number from sample and record or correct it below.]

(__ __ __)__ __ __-__ __ __ __

Thank you for your time! We look forward to seeing you on July 16, at [time selected above].

Interviewer:

Record Gender: 1. Female 2. Male

Communications Focus Group
Focus Group Screener

Date: __ __/__ __/__ __

Call Start: __ __:__ __ Call End: __ __:__ __

Interviewer ID#: __ __ __ __

Phone: (__ __ __)__ __ __-__ __ __ __

[Ask to speak with male head of household.]

Hello, my name is _____ with **(1) Focus, Inc., a local marketing research firm.** We are conducting **(2) a study among area residents concerning communications** and would appreciate your input. **(3) We are *not* selling anything** and will only take a few minutes of your time. **(4) All of your responses will be kept confidential.**

S1. First, are you between the ages of 18 and 39?

> 1. Yes [indicate age: __ __; continue to **S2**]
>
> 2. No [thank and terminate]
>
> 3. Refused [thank and terminate]

S2. Was your last year's household income before taxes between $25,000 and $40,000?

> 1. No [thank and terminate]
>
> 2. Yes [continue to **S3**]

3. Don't know/refused [thank and terminate]

S3. What is your ethnic background? [probe if needed]

1. Hispanic [continue if group 1 not full; otherwise thank and terminate]

2. Caucasian [continue if group 2 not full; otherwise thank and terminate]

3. Asian-American [continue if group 2 not full; otherwise thank and terminate]

4. African-American [continue if group 2 not full; otherwise thank and terminate]

5. Other [continue if group 2 not full; otherwise thank and terminate]

6. Refused [thank and terminate]

S4. Do you *personally* own a cellular phone?

1. Yes [thank and terminate]

2. No [continue to S5]

3. Refused [thank and terminate]

S5. (5) Do you or does anyone in your household work in a communications field (phone company, cellular company, etc.) or advertising or marketing research firm?

1. Yes [thank and terminate]

2. No [continue to S6]

3. Don't know/refused [thank and terminate]

S6. (6) Have you attended a focus group discussion within the past 6 months?

    1. Yes [thank and terminate]

    2. No [continue to **S7**]

S7. Do you currently own a pager?

    1. Yes

    2. No

S8. Focus, Inc. will be conducting a focus group discussion on Wednesday, May 27, at Focus Inc. in Anytown. The discussion will center on your own communication needs, and no sales will be involved. The session will last approximately 90 minutes, and refreshments will be served. In addition, **(8) you will receive $40 for your participation. (7) Would you be interested in attending this group?**

    1. Yes [complete participant information section, then provide appropriate time and directions based on quota group; if participant is unsure, schedule callback]

    2. No [thank and terminate]

    3. Don't know [schedule callback]

Participant Information:

So that we can send you a confirmation letter and directions to the group, I need your full name and mailing address:

Name: _____

Address: _____

City/State: _____ Zip: _____

Also, I would like to confirm that the phone number at which I reached you is: [Read number from sample and record or correct it below.]

(__ __ __)__ __ __-__ __ __ __

Thank you for your time! We look forward to seeing you on Wednesday, May 27, at [6 or 8 P.M. dependent on quota group filled].

Software Study
Focus Group Screener

Date: __ __/__ __/__ __

Interviewer ID#: __ __ __ __

[Initially ask to speak with a customer service representative or a collection agent—use title most appropriate based on firm being contacted. After reaching that person, begin with complete introduction:]

Hello, my name is _____ with **(1) ABC Research** in Chicago. We are conducting a **(2) research study with persons such as yourself who have frequent telephone customer contacts. (3) We are *not* selling anything** and will take only a moment of your time. [If contact is unable to talk during work hours, ask if he or she can be called at home. If so, get name/phone number for callback. If not, thank and terminate.]

S1. In your position, do you spend at least 50 percent of your time making outbound and/or handling inbound customer calls while using a computer terminal to obtain the related customer records?

　　1. Yes [continue to **S2**]

　　2. No [thank and terminate]

　　3. Don't know/refused [thank and terminate]

S2. (5) Do you or does anyone in your household work for a software design firm, an advertising agency, or a marketing research firm?

 1. Yes [thank and terminate]

 2. No [continue to **S3**]

 3. Don't know/refused [thank and terminate]

S3. (6) Have you participated in a focus group study within the past 6 months?

 1. Yes [thank and terminate]

 2. No [continue to **S4**]

 3. Don't know/refused [thank and terminate]

S4. We will be conducting a focus group discussion with customer contact personnel such as yourself. The discussion will center on a new software product related to your field. The purpose of the group is solely to obtain your opinions, and all of **(4) your comments will be kept confidential.** The session will last about 1 hour and 45 minutes. Refreshments will be served, and **(8) you will also be paid $35 for your participation. (7) Would you be interested in attending this group?**

 1. Yes [continue to **S3**]

 2. No [thank and terminate]

 3. Don't know/refused [thank and terminate]

S5. The group is scheduled for 6:00 P.M. on Monday, September 25, at ABC Research. Will you be able to join us?

    1. Yes [continue to information]

    2. Possibly [arrange callback]

    3. No [thank and terminate]

    4. Refused [thank and terminate]

Participant Information:

[Provide respondent with general facility location if needed.]

So that we can send you a confirmation letter and directions to the group, I need your full name and the appropriate mailing address. We also need your position/title: [Even if mailing is going to home address, note that company name should be included. Indicate if this is home or business address so confirmation letter adds/deletes title and company name accordingly.]

Circle one: 1. Home address   2. Business address

Name: _____

Title: _____

Company: _____

Mailing Address: _____

City/State: _____ Zip: _____

Also, I would like to confirm that the phone number I reached you at is: [Read number from sample and record or correct it below. Add extension if applicable.]

(__ __ __)__ __ __-__ __ __ __ Extension: __ __ __ __

Thank you for your time! We look forward to seeing you at 6:00 P.M. on September 25.

Sample Focus Group Discussion Guides

The three samples in this appendix are typical of focus group discussion guides. The guides are presented in outline form. To the left of the outline are recommended amounts of time to spend discussing each topic.

For a discussion of how to develop discussion guides, see Chapter 2. In addition, Chapter 4 explores how to use these guides.

Water Quality
Focus Group Discussion Guide

(10 min.) Introduction

- Greeting

- Purpose of focus groups

- Opportunity to offer opinions/input about several ads

- Ground rules

  - Role of moderator

  - Recording equipment/one-way mirror

  - Confidentiality of comments (no right or wrong)

  - Note that co-op is for *time*, not for your *answers*

  - Speak one at a time and as clearly as possible

- Brief get-acquainted period—names/occupations/hobbies

- Explain that we will be looking at *concepts* (beginning stage of the ads)—consider the idea rather than looking at these as final ads

(15 min.) Concept 1

- Presentation of storyboard

- Initial reactions? Why? Likes/dislikes?

- What is the message or point of the ad(s)? What did you learn?

(15 min.) Concept 2 (put 1 aside for now)

- Presentation of storyboard

- Initial reactions? Why? Likes/dislikes?

- What is the message or point of the ad(s)? What did you learn?

(15 min.) Concept 3 (put 2 aside for now)

- Presentation of storyboard

- Initial reactions? Why? Likes/dislikes?

- What is the message or point of the ad(s)? What did you learn?

(5 min.) Break

(15 min.) Determining Preferred Concept

- Place all storyboards in front of group
  - Which one would, in your opinion, have the greatest effect on water quality awareness in your community?
    - Why?

- Which one would be most likely to make you think about and/or alter your own behavior?

  - Why?

- Which one do you believe will be most effective overall?

  - Why?

  - Least effective?

  - Why?

- Other comments regarding the ads?

(10 min.) Reaction to Logo Options

- Briefly explain what the logo is for.

- Present logo options.

  - Which one do you prefer? Why?

  - General likes/dislikes regarding each? Why?

- Other comments regarding the logos?

(5 min.) Closing Comments

- Any additional comments?

- Thank participants and remind them to pick up co-op payments.

Acme Credit Union Senior Package Account Focus Group Discussion Guide

(10 min.) Introduction

- Greeting

- Purpose of focus group

  - Opportunity to discuss financial services/your banking needs

- Ground rules

  - Role of moderator

  - Recording groups

  - Confidentiality of comments (not asking account balance information)

  - Individual opinions (no right or wrong)

  - Speak one at a time and as clearly as possible

(10 min.) Customers' Lifestyles

- Are you currently retired?

  - If not, when do you anticipate retiring?

- What do you see as positive aspects of retirement for you personally? (e.g., travel, hobbies, time with family)

- What potential problems do you think of in connection

with your (pending) retirement? (e.g., health/medical, fixed income)

(10 min.) Financial Services Usage

- How long have you been with Acme Credit Union?

  - Is it your primary financial institution?

    - If not, which one is?

- What types of products/services do you have with Acme Credit Union?

  - With other institutions?

- Are your needs being met in terms of products/services?

  - Are there other products/services that you could use?

- How effective is Acme Credit Union in terms of communication with its customers?

  - How could communications be improved?

(10 min.) Package Accounts (General Awareness)

- Are you familiar with package accounts? (unaided/aided)

- Have you ever had one (at any institution)?

  - If yes, what was included in the package? Cost?

- Are you familiar with any packages for the 55+ age group?

- If yes, who offers it? What does it include? What is it called?

(5 min.) Break

(30 min.) Senior Package Features/Requirements

- Are you interested in such a seniors' package?

  - If no, why not?

  - If yes, what benefits/services should it include? (top of mind)

- Which services would you be likely to use/not use? (show Phase I list)

  - Why/why not?

- Other services might also be considered . . . (show Phase II/III lists)

  - Interested? Likely to use?

    - Why/why not?

- What retirement-related information should be included?

- Such packages generally have product or balance requirements for eligibility . . . (show flip chart)

  - Considering Senior Checking/Money Market/CD as requirements:

- Reasonable requirements?

- Given the services, benefits, and rates we've discussed, would you open accounts or consolidate funds from other institutions to get this package?

  - Why/why not?

(10 min.) Senior Package Name

- If it were your job to market this package, what would you name it? (unaided)

- Should it be referred to as a "club" or a "group"?

  - Why/why not?

- Would any of the following names be appropriate? (show list)

  - Why/why not?

(5 min.) Closing Comments

- If you could give one suggestion to the credit union's president about developing a seniors' package account, what would it be?

- Thank participants and remind them to pick up co-op fee on way out.

Communications Focus Group Discussion Guide

(5 min.) Introduction

- Greeting

- Purpose of focus groups

- Ground rules

  - Role of moderator

  - Recording equipment

  - Confidentiality of comments

  - No right or wrong answers

  - Speak one at a time and loud and clear

- Brief get-acquainted period (names/occupations)

(10 min.) General Familiarity with Cell Phone/Airtime Offers

- Understand from recruiting that none of you personally own a cellular phone. Do you use one at work? Type? What provider is airtime through?

- Have you ever personally had a cellular phone before? When?

  - If yes, who was the airtime provider?

- If no, have you ever considered one?

  - If no, why not?

- Pros/cons of phones/airtime used at work/personally?

(10 min.) Pager Usage

- Do you have/use a pager?

  - Type?

- Use primarily for personal or business purposes?

- How did you select your pager? (i.e., how did you choose the company? ad/recommendation/experience?)

- Why did you choose a pager versus a cellular phone?

- Do more of your friends/co-workers have pagers than have cellular phones?

  - Why/why not?

(10 min.) Perceived Benefits of Cellular Phones

- Have you ever considered getting a cellular phone?

  - If yes, why were you considering it?

  - If no, why haven't you considered it?

- If you personally had a cellular phone now, what would you use it for? (probe: work, emergencies, family use, travel, convenience)

- What is the main reason that you do not personally have a cellular phone now?

  - Other reasons?

(5 min.) Airtime Provider Awareness/Perceived Image

- How important would the company you purchase cellular airtime from be to you?

- What airtime providers are you aware of? (list)

  - Which company is most reliable/has best reputation?

  - Which is most/least expensive?

- Have you ever used any of these companies for any service?

- Does the size of the company matter to you?

  - Why/why not?

(10 min.) Media Profile

- Television

  - How many of you watch TV regularly?

    - What channel(s) most frequently? Times?

    - Types of shows? (probe)

- Radio

  - Do you listen to the radio regularly?

- What station(s) most frequently? Times?

- Print

  - What newspapers do you read regularly?

    - Specific sections or skim? (probe)

(10 min.) General Opinions Re: Phone Ads

- What ads have you seen related to phones/long distance/cellular?

  - Could you determine what they were selling?

    - Why/why not?

- What catches your eye in these types of ads? What turns you off? (e.g., does a picture of a phone in an ad turn you off?)

  - Why/why not?

(10 min.) Ad Concept Testing

- Show/play advertisements and discuss perceived messages/likes and dislikes:

  - Radio

  - Television

  - Print

- What benefits do you see from the program as shown in the ads?

- (After ads viewed) Can you name the company sponsoring the ads?

  - Why/why not?

(10 min.) Program Evaluation

- Briefly explain proposed package:

  - Interest levels? Why?

  - Likes/dislikes? Why?

  - What would increase their interest level?

(5 min.) Closing Comments

- Has your interest in a cellular phone changed since the beginning of the group?

  - Why/why not?

- Additional comments/input?

- Thank participants and remind them to pick up co-op payments on way out.

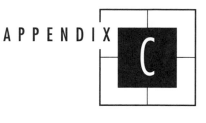

Sample Executive Summary Reports

Following are several examples of summary reports based on actual focus group studies. Do not rely on any data presented herein; the report samples are provided only as fictionalized examples of how focus group reports are formatted and how the qualitative results of groups are analyzed. To protect confidentiality, the names of the clients and vendors have been changed, and all of the reports are several years old at the time of this book's release. Dates, quotations, and conclusions have also been changed extensively, and specific concepts discussed are not included in detail.

Each of these reports is associated with screener questionnaires and discussion guides appearing as examples in Appendixes A and B. Those documents have also been revised to maintain confidentiality.

Water Quality

FOCUS GROUP STUDY

Executive Summary Report

Contents

Introduction
Background Information

Methodology

Key Insights

Executive Summary
Participants' Awareness of Water Quality

Advertising Concept Testing

Preferred Advertising Concept

Logo Evaluations

,nd Information

Quantai.. Research Specialists was commissioned by XYZ Advertising Agency to conduct two focus groups of Anytown area residents to test advertising and logo concepts for the County Water Quality Board. The study had the following specific objectives:

- Determination of participants' comprehension of the advertisements' messages

- Assessment of the advertisements' appeal in terms of both their concepts and messages

- Evaluation of potential behavior changes attributed to each advertisement

- Identification of the preferred logo option for the County Water Quality Board

Methodology

Two focus groups were conducted with Anytown area residents (from Brown, Connor, and Green Counties). Participants were randomly recruited by telephone, utilizing the services of a marketing research subcontractor. Participants were screened to be heads of households and between the ages of twenty-five and fifty-four. Additional screening questions ensured that they were not employed by advertising agencies or environmental firms. Approximately half of all group participants were homeowners. Persons of diverse ethnic backgrounds participated in each group.

The focus groups were conducted at Qualitative Research Specialists' focus group facility on the evening of Wednesday, June 20. Both groups were audio- and videotaped for reporting purposes. All participants received a co-op fee for their time.

Key Insights

- Residents are familiar with oil as a source of water quality problems, but not as familiar with how auto oil leaks *reach* the water. They are even less familiar with other causes of water pollution such as fertilizers, car washing, pet wastes, and bikes in the watershed. The topics addressed in the ad concepts are providing them with new information, but they need it carried one step further. Instead of simply pointing out the problem, they want the solution more clearly defined in all of the advertisements: What are the alternatives to chemical fertilizers? What should they do with the pet waste? Where should they dispose of their oil?

- Participants *strongly* favored ad concept 2 in both its print and its television formats. Many of them did, however, have difficulties visualizing two million gallons and believed substituting an oil tanker in the example would be more effective. It was also suggested that this concept should be carried further, with additional ads covering other water pollution problems such as fertilizers and pet wastes.

- While participants preferred ad concept 2, they *learned* the most from ad concept 1. They were put on the defensive by the idea that each individual is contributing to water pollution—so much so that several of them balked and asked why the advertisements do not target corporations, the "real" perpetrators of the pollution. The animation caught their attention, but the language and "innuendos" were considered somewhat offensive and extreme.

- Television concept 3 "lost" most of the participants, as did its accompanying print advertisement. Participants had to spend too much time getting past what they saw to the actual message, and they often missed the message altogether. They were overly concerned with the gender issue that arose from having only men in the advertisement. In the print ad, most participants simply did not understand how the bicycle contributed to water pollution, and several were also concerned that the ad portrayed children in a negative manner.

- In terms of the logos tested, participants liked both the oval version and the "water ripple" version. While the oval logo said "quality" and "authority" to many, those favoring the ripple logo preferred its more distinctive appearance. Several suggested that if some color were added to the ripple to emphasize the water image, they too would select that logo.

Executive Summary
Participants' Awareness of Water Quality

In both groups, participants were asked to complete a brief questionnaire to provide a profile of their own levels of awareness regarding water quality in the Anytown area. Initially, they were asked to rate the water quality in Anytown on a five-point scale (1 = poor; 5 = excellent). (Remember that focus groups are qualitative, so these numbers provide only a guideline versus statistically valid survey results.) Overall, Group I gave an average rating of 3.00, while Group II's average rating was only slightly higher at 3.36. Following are the individual reasons given for each of the ratings:

GROUP I

"They are putting things into water now that won't show until later, and the damage will already [be] done."

"My family and I do a lot of nature walking and beach-combing, and so much of the water is mucky and full of garbage."

"Where I grew up, the lake was so polluted; there were no fish, and no one went in the water! That's polluted! People here are much more aware of water quality than in other parts of the country."

"The water here in comparison to the water where I came from is like night and day. You do not have to purchase water purification equipment."

"Drinking water is very bad—fluoride, depletions of our natural resources of fish."

"I have experienced living and visiting other areas and make my rating on the basis of a comparison to those areas."

"We're doing pretty well now, but the system is starting to be impacted by more and more people in the same size space."

<u>GROUP II</u>

"Whenever I am around the water, I see lots of garbage floating in it."

"My experiences are from living elsewhere, where often the water is filled with sand or rust or lime."

"Our water is not hard as in other areas in which I've lived, nor is it tainted by pollutants. . . ."

"It could be better in some areas, probably most areas, but overall is much better than some places I've seen."

"Comparative relationship—Anytown water quality versus other areas, which I view as poor."

"H_2O out of my faucet is often yellow or orange; needed to buy a filter; seafood is contaminated."

"Streams, lakes in my area have appeared clean when I have visited or gone swimming in them; clear, not much debris or garbage."

"Because half of the time it tastes like rust and smells like bleach."

"Because much of our water needs to be treated due to pollution . . ."

"Having traveled across the United States, I feel Anytown's water tastes the best. As far as I know, it's pretty pure."

Participants cited a number of causes of water pollution in their own neighborhoods, including improper disposal of motor oil, oil leaks, washing cars, dumping garbage near water, animal wastes, local sewage treatment plants, lawn chemicals and fertilizers, and paint disposal. One person suggested that when the utility company or fire department runs any local hydrant, sediments appear in his water. In each group, there was one participant who did not see *any* sources of water pollution in his or her neighborhood.

In terms of their own efforts to protect water quality, they offered a number of examples. Most mentioned proper disposal of oil (particularly in terms of having oil professionally changed), minimizing fertilizer use or using organic fertilizers, using less hazardous cleaning solutions, and proper disposal of other household chemicals. A few also cited cleaning up pet wastes.

Advertising Concept Testing

Three advertising concepts were presented to each group. The presentation itself consisted solely of showing the storyboards and reading the related copy to the participants. Care was taken to avoid any tone that could be interpreted as "selling" the participants regarding any of the advertisements. Each concept (television and print at the same time) was presented separately from the others and discussed immediately following its presentation. Later the participants were allowed to make comparisons and identify their preferences among all three concepts. To reduce the potential for bias based on presentation order, the concepts were presented in a different order to each of the two groups.

Concept 1: Print Advertisement

Participants' initial comments regarding the print advertisement for this concept emphasized their concerns about the copy in particular, as well as some disbelief about the effects of pet waste on water quality. In addition, there was some confusion regarding who specifically (children versus adults) this advertisement would be targeting.

"I'm not sure I like this. I think some of the phrasing on this . . . print ad bothers me. . . . This to me appears to be directed to kids in general, and . . . I have a problem with the print ad, I really do."

"I think I agree; the use of all the little asides; they don't really make a lot of sense. . . ."

". . . Personally, I just don't like cutesy cartoons. . . . I probably personally wouldn't read it."

"I like the cutesy ads . . . but this one's confusing because of the phrasing."

"It's hard enough to get people to pick up litter . . . so . . . it's good for the information . . . the point is good. . . ."

"I agree . . . about the phrasing of the print ad. It seems that the phrasing is aimed at adults, and I'd be really upset if that kind of phrasing was geared at kids because of the mixed messages. . . . That's . . . inappropriate."

"It rubbed me the wrong way, too."

"That bothers me, too . . . totally inappropriate."

"I like the fact . . . just because I have a pet and . . . I didn't realize this . . . that makes me want to pick it up all the time. . . ."

"Neither did I [realize about effect]."

". . . gets me mad. . . . I can't imagine that much pet waste period, so I just question where do they pull a fact like that from. . . . where do they get their statistics? . . . I have just never heard that before, so it's kind of new. . . . I just discredit the whole thing."

". . . I had a dog for years, and where she had her doghouse, the grass was beautiful and green . . . natural fertilizer . . ."

"It really seems like a natural fertilizer. I know back home on the farm . . . we would spray that stuff in the fields. . . ."

"I thought it was aimed more at schoolchildren. . . . I don't know if it's the cartoon drawing, but some of it is so simple and basic that it seems it's something that would be taught to the kids in school. . . ."

". . . This one really depends on where it's going to be run.
. . . It's an awfully simplistic style with a pretty heavy
message. . . ."

"The only [thing] that makes sense about that . . . you get
the idea . . . these are going to be a series . . . but still . . ."

Some participants in the second group questioned why the
advertisement does not go a step further and explain where you
should dispose of the pet wastes:

". . . I also think if they're going to talk about pet wastes,
then once they put it in the Baggie, where are they going to
put it? . . ."

"I agree. . . . What are we supposed to do with it?"

". . . If you put it in the garbage can, it ends up in the land-
fill and ends up in the water anyway . . ."

Concept 1: Television Advertisement

Participants were *somewhat* more receptive of the television advertisement, although it was viewed as a bit simplistic and somewhat
of a "scare tactic" in terms of its copy. Again, it was seen as possibly
being intended to target kids, as most adults have heard these messages repeatedly. Some comments indicated concern that large companies should be targeted with such advertising, rather than
individuals, since that is where they believe the major pollution
problems originate.

"This type of thing doesn't cause the major pollution problems . . . the major big companies . . . I see that they're pointing at each one of us, and I don't think each one of us does as much pollution as a big company. I don't know if they're directing it at the right people."

"This theme . . . seems to be for a younger audience than adults. . . ."

"Yeah, they gotta run it on Saturday morning with the cartoons, the video side of it."

". . . We have gotten so much information about the environment and the things that you do that affect the environment, that this is a very *simplistic* message for us . . . so I don't see that it's doing that good of job of educating. . . ."

"But if it's geared toward children . . . these are the sorts of things that as your kids see you doing them, if they have seen these ads . . . then they kind of remind you about, 'Well, you're not supposed to do that; it's bad for the environment.'"

"I like that one in general . . . it gets the point across."

". . . The TV ad plays on one of my pet peeves. . . . They're doing it again, they're scaring the kids! It just seems to me like they're saying, 'We're going to pollute the whole world, and we're not going to have any nice places anymore . . . you'd better be worried . . .'"

"The phrase . . . 'It's dangerous and full of awful things'; that might be overstated . . . scaring kids; if indeed this is intended for a juvenile audience; I'm not so sure it is . . . I think it might be a bit extreme."

". . . They need to do some changing in the wording, especially if they're going to aim it at kids."

". . . If you're gonna wash it [your car] in front of your house or at a car wash, it's still gonna go down the sewers . . . but, overall, I think I like that one. I think some of the wording could be different . . . maybe about the car . . . the vocabulary could be different. . . . It kind of loses you with the wording. . . ."

Participants did, however, generally grasp a message from this ad that individuals can have an effect on water quality:

"So the theme is that these are the everyday things that people can do that cause pollution as distinct from . . . industry pollution. . . . So I guess the idea is to appeal . . . to people in the sense of 'These are things that you can do to affect the environment'. . ."

"That's how I see it, too, 'cause I haven't seen nothing in the ad about any chemicals, heavy chemicals, like what companies would do. . . . [This is] the human standpoint."

". . . It seems to me that that is part of what they're trying to do is educate, and maybe these notions that we have that it is the corporate polluters that are doing all the

damage is inaccurate; maybe the idea that we as individuals are doing as much; we have the potential to do as
much damage to the environment as a corporate entity
would."

"What I like about the TV ad is it shows how easily we inad-
vertently pollute the water. I think that's very important."

As with the print version of this concept, participants pointed
out the need to compare and contrast—to show not just what *not* to
do, but to also show either the results of polluting or how to avoid
polluting:

"A before-and-after kind of thing."

"I like this one better. . . . I think . . . in a positive way to
tell people what *to do* rather than saying what *not* to do. . . .
They also need to know what they *should* do . . ."

". . . it's all things that we know, but . . . where does it go
from there? . . . If it's still pretty and nice, it's not going to
make an impact of what it does to the environment, because
they're showing it still in its pretty state . . ."

"There's something he left out . . . where the water is right
there, why didn't he have a picture where they have fish
where the water was clean, fish swimming in the dirty
water? . . ."

". . . it's not teaching us anything new. There needs to be a
comparison and contrast."

". . . A lot of people have the attitude 'Well, this is geared toward individuals, where big corporations cause the most pollution.' I think if they could incorporate a way . . . to show the damage of people constantly dropping oil in the ground . . . the amount that it really does, so it can kind of show that one individual *can* contribute to a lot of [pollution] . . ."

". . . It would've been nice to interject a little picture that would . . . show somebody washing their car through a car-wash, disposing of oil properly . . . showing the alternatives that we want people to use. . . ."

Several participants in the first group also indicated that the animation aspect of the ad could possibly be an "attention getter":

"I liked that aspect of it for television."

"I'd probably look at it, yes."

"I'd be curious; it's different."

Concept 2: Television and Print Advertisements

With the second concept, participants discussed the print and tele-vision advertisements in conjunction with each other, possibly because the ads covered the same issue in both formats, unlike Con-cept 1. They all *knew* that oil is a problem in terms of its effect on water quality, but felt that these advertisements emphasized the extent of the problem. They liked how the ads show that each indi-

vidual can contribute to the solution. As noted with the first concept, however, they felt that the impact of the pollution should be
illustrated in the ads—show *how* the oil is polluting the water.

"I like it."

". . . I guess my concern about it is I'm not sure it provides
enough information. . . . I think that it's good that it clarifies
what the impact is . . . but it would be more powerful to me
if it said, . . . 'The oil tanker spilled whatever.'. . . The point
is that some catastrophe that everybody . . . knows about . . .
and which is rare, gets all the attention, but the impact of
something that happens every single day . . . to me that's a
very powerful image . . ."

"Much better . . . I think the simplicity of the message. It's
a little easier, clearer. . . . It's short, too. . . ."

"I do like this one. . . . I still would like these ads to somewhere show the impact on, how about the fish? . . . that we
do eat the fish after they swim in the oil . . ."

". . . The 'dispose of the oil properly,' what's that? *How* do
you dispose of oil properly?"

". . . The leaks; I guess when a car's traveling on a highway
is when it leaks, so rains come; that's why it goes in a storm
drain, and that's where the water isn't treated right . . . that
would be an idea—to start with one car, show a freeway
scene in a traffic jam . . . more educational."

". . . It's kind of hard to fathom; I think of my car, 'OK, it might have an oil leak,' but I don't really take my car out in the woods and stuff . . . show the *process* . . ."

"I like it. . . . It got my attention; the fact about what the oil is doing to the water, contaminating it . . . over the years the damage is going to show up in people's bodies."

"My other concern is, sure, we all know that that does happen, but I would like to see a message like 'Call a number.' What are we supposed to do with the oil? . . ."

"Sounds like something I've heard five billion times already."

"I think it's effective."

"I do, too, because it's always about *ships* leaking oil; you never hear about cars."

"We're talking about *one* drop of oil making a difference, not a ship leaking nor somebody dumping a whole can of oil down a storm drain . . ."

". . . It shows how just a little bit has such a major effect on the environment."

"I like the concept due to the fact that each individual can do something about the solution."

". . . It's something I can do about it instead of like the major oil spills."

"It's a good ad, I think. The *concept* is good. Again, in a lot of respects . . . it's the same thing I've heard in a lot of cases about not dumping your garbage . . . and a lot of people might just let it go in one ear and out the other . . ."

"We're powerless to stop the tankers from leaking, but we're *not* powerless to stop the leaks from our cars."

"Hopefully, if they're doing one like this, they'll follow up with other things besides the oil damaging the water . . ."

Many felt that a statistic related to an oil tanker would be more effective in this advertisement:

"I have no concept of what a gallon is, believe it or not, but I have a fairly good idea of what an oil tanker looks like."

"When you said 'oil tanker,' I was thinking, 'Does she mean a truck, a ship, a railcar?'. . . I'd like to see a picture of it . . ."

Concept 3: Print Advertisement

The print ad for the third concept confused participants. While they ultimately could *derive* reasons why kids should not ride their bicycles through streams, they felt that this was a minor issue. They wanted the ad to tell them how this affects water quality. Several also commented that the advertisement seems to portray children in a negative manner:

"I never thought about kids riding back and forth through a stream. I've seen kids do that lots of times . . ."

". . . I'd like to know *how* that destroys water quality . . ."

"It doesn't really explain why."

"Yeah, it doesn't [explain why]."

"All it tells me is 'Don't let your kids play in the streams on their bikes'. . ."

"My *guess* why they don't want them riding through a stream would be the rubber in the tires and the oil . . ."

"I'm offended by the negativism directed toward our children again. That just rubs me the wrong way. My children are disciplined and loved; they do *not* destroy the house, and that personally offends me."

". . . I just couldn't see where a child riding through a stream . . . even if he decides to ride through back and forth over and over again would be so harmful that it would merit that much attention . . ."

". . . I don't know why the bike is polluting the water."

"I think that what they may be shooting for is just the fact that riding through the stream hurts the watershed."

"Like how many kids really do that?"

". . . We live right near a watershed . . . and the kids don't even get in it . . ."

"With the bicycle one, . . . I would think that there would be a large segment of the audience that would not relate to that at all, because my kids would never have the opportunity to be riding in some stream . . ."

"It's just so small of a population that takes their bikes in the water . . . It's a very narrow audience."

". . . I just don't see where that *conveys* anything . . ."

Concept 3: Television Advertisement

While participants chuckled a bit when the television ad was presented, most got too tied up in the individual features of the ad (the poem, the "sameness," etc.) that the message of the advertisement seemed to be lost:

"It seems like I'd be sort of distracted . . ."

"I didn't think that fertilizer was . . . harmful. . . . I wouldn't understand that would've been bad . . ."

"I think you would be better off having someone walk through a neighborhood where people are doing various activities on a Saturday morning . . . a dad, his kids, and a neighbor . . . and you see the guy changing the oil and letting the oil slop all over and dumping it right down the sewer . . . using fertilizers and then having the father commenting on what's wrong with that."

". . . I see women even more involved than men in fertilizing . . . it's kind of half and half and not just men . . ."

". . . I think it would take people a long time to figure out what you're really trying to say and then the guilt of watering your lawn after you used a pesticide on it . . ."

"I have a difficult time kind of relating to this notion of the *sameness* . . . I don't know . . . what the message is . . ."

"It's done in a silly manner, and the idea . . . takes away from the seriousness of the point they're trying to bring across . . ."

"I thought it [the poem] was condescending . . ."

"I don't like the poem either . . ."

"It seems like the entire thrust of the whole thing . . . is the idea that we as individuals can make a difference, one individual at a time. . . . The video just seems a little simplistic . . ."

"I liked this concept because it was very succinct; it was to the point, and it only covered one possible form of pollution. I would like to see a number of these types of things for each type of pollution."

"Women buy fertilizer; women fertilize lawns."

"It didn't move me one way or the other. . . . I thought the poetry was cute, but . . . I don't think it would motivate me . . . in how I care for the environment."

"It's different . . . I think people need education. I think we need to learn about all these things somehow . . ."

In the second group, where participants discussed concerns about gender representation in this ad, they were asked if men *and* women appearing in the advertisement would work better. The group ultimately agreed that it would still be workable if one version of the ad used only men and then the next ad used all women.

Preferred Advertising Concept

Television Advertisements

In terms of the advertisements' effectiveness in raising water quality awareness in their community, participants in both groups overwhelmingly favored Concept 2 for the television format. Regarding the television ads' potential to change their *own* behaviors, most also believed that this concept would be the most effective. Some did, however, note that Concept 1 actually imparted more information, just not as effectively. Again, participants stressed the need for the addition of some cause-and-effect illustrations.

> "I like number 2 the best. . . . Number 1 has the most information, but I don't think number 1 is necessarily effective."

> ". . . I think the reason I like number 2 the best is it's short, it's sweet, it's to the point, and it . . . hits home really fast . . ."

> "I also agree that number 2 is short and to the point. I think it's more realistic. . . . It's more of 'An individual person can do something about it'. . ."

"Again, I already make sure my car doesn't leak . . . but I'd forgotten about washing the car, and if I fertilize, I'd sure think about it, and when my husband changes the oil next time, I'll go out there and watch him. . . . I think that number 1 would change my behavior just because it's more information."

"Number 2 gets to the point; easy."

Print Advertisements

Participants in both groups preferred Concept 2 in the print advertisement as well, although in terms of affecting their personal behavior, most in the second group felt that they had learned more from Concept 1.

"Number 2 . . . I love that ad. . . . I like number 1 though, too . . . because that's something I hadn't known . . ."

"Probably number 1 because I didn't realize . . . I have a dog . . ."

"I'd say number 2 would have the greatest impact. . . . If you walk through a parking lot, you're always stepping over oil. Oil is everywhere in the environment, and maybe that would have an impact, I don't know."

". . . What I see as a very big difference between numbers 1 and 2 . . . you have someone in number 1 telling you you should always pick up after your pet; she's telling you what to do. In number 2 no one is telling you what to do; it's like you're figuring it out by yourself . . ."

Logo Evaluations

Four potential logos for the County Water Quality Board were also presented to the participants in both focus groups. For analytical purposes, the logos will be referred to as follows:

> 1 [oval around the name]
>
> 2 [name with "waves" under the word *water*]
>
> 3 [name with "water ripple"]
>
> 4 [name without illustration]

Group I favored Logo 1, while the second group preferred Logo 3. Following are their comments regarding each of the logos:

<u>LOGO 1</u>

". . . I was going to critique number 1; that looks to me like a warning label . . . or it looks like a generic label."

"The first one I was thinking that it could be anything. . . . It's not distinctive for water quality."

". . . I definitely don't like number 1 . . ."

"On number 1, I liked that at first. I like the fact that it says 'quality' to me . . ."

"I like 1 and 3 equally. . . . I'd go back and put number 1 in a water drop."

"You could take number 1 and turn it sideways and make it look like a raindrop and put stuff inside of it."

"I think the oval is so neat because it reminds me of a 1950s commercial . . . simple and cleaner . . ."

"It's conservative and authoritative . . ."

". . . That stands out . . . it's solid, it's easy to read . . ."

LOGO 2

"I like the second one with the blue waves; the idea is clean water . . . the idea that you want the water quality from what it is today to become pure, clear . . . the idea of blue . . ."

"Number 2, I really like the colors; the colors catch my eye and draw me to it."

". . . I think number 2, I want the letters to be closer together or something . . . it is so spread out . . ."

"I like the font type, and I like the little waves. . . . Number 1 was my second choice, however. I could see both of these being used in different campaigns. I could see number 1 being used as a stamp of approval at the end of something and number 2 in script somewhere."

LOGO 3

"I thought of the water . . ."

"It could be something that they could use . . . when people see that they should automatically know what it stands for . . ."

"I kind of like number 3, but a lot of people would probably be wondering, 'What is that thing?'. . ."

". . . It looks like a ripple of water. . . . I'd have to go with number 3."

". . . I like number 3 because it's something unique . . ."

"I like number 3 . . . because it reminds me of a puddle of water."

"I like number 3. From a distance, that one just catches my eye the most . . ."

"I think for catching your eye, I like number 3 the best; in terms of printing that stands out . . . this almost looks like a stove burner . . . but I think of the four I'd pick number 3."

"I think I like number 3, but I would put some color into the puddle; some blue. . . . That black and white kind of makes it look . . . like a burner or whatever . . ."

"If number 3 had some color rather than just the black, I could go for that easily."

LOGO 4

". . . I definitely don't like number 4 . . ."

"It looks like a law firm."

". . . The fourth one, I've seen that before."

". . . Number 4, and only because, to me, I want something in a print ad that I have to look at, not necessarily something that's going to just jump right out at me . . . that's just clean-cut and precise."

Acme Credit Union

SENIOR PROGRAM FOCUS GROUPS

Executive Summary Report

Contents

Introduction
Background

Methodology

Recommendations

Executive Summary
Financial Institution Usage

    Relationships with ACU

    Affiliations with Other Institutions

    Primary Financial Institution

Personal Contact with Staff

Attitudes Toward Automated Services

Lifestyle Issues

General Attitudes Toward Senior Programs

Senior Program Features

Eligibility and Pricing

Member Suggestions

Introduction

Background

Focus Scope Research was commissioned by Acme Credit Union (ACU) to conduct a focus group study to determine senior members' financial product/service needs. The purpose of the study is to provide ACU with the information necessary to develop the most appropriate senior program for its market. The study had three specific objectives:

- Determining what types of products/services senior members need or anticipate future needs for

- Identifying seniors' price expectations for needed products/services

- Determining likelihood of new product/service success based on member input

Methodology

Two focus groups were conducted with Acme Credit Union members aged fifty and over. Participants were randomly recruited from a list of senior members, which was provided by the credit union. Recruiting was conducted by telephone utilizing the professional interviewing services of Focus Scope Research. Members were screened to confirm their age and that they are responsible (or share responsibility) for their household's financial business. In addition, potential participants were screened to ensure that they are not employees or board members of any financial institution.

Twelve qualified seniors were scheduled per group. Eight arrived and participated in each group. The focus groups were held on July 16 at Focus Scope Research's focus group facility in Anytown. Groups lasted approximately ninety minutes and were video- and audiotaped for reporting purposes. All participants received co-op payments of $30.

Recommendations

- ACU members would welcome a senior program provided that it would include free checking and check printing, savings, free traveler's checks, free notary service, a no-fee credit card, a debit/ATM card, free money orders and cashier's checks, and seminars. These products/services would have to be the base of a package to interest seniors.

- In addition to the preceding products/services, consider offering safe-deposit boxes, discounted loan rates, and competitive interest on checking accounts with a minimum balance. Other benefits in which seniors expressed interest included the services of a financial adviser, travel benefits (tours/discounts), prescription and eyewear discounts, and free funds transfers. The key is the emphasis on low-cost or (better yet) free benefits. The participants are all cost-conscious and look for "deals."

- Seniors are also concerned with convenience but would prefer convenience with a "human side." While many use the automated teller machines or telephone banking service, most would rather talk to an actual person at the credit union.

Given time and convenience issues, however, many of them simply cannot get to one of the branches when they need to conduct a transaction, and they have to rely on the automated services. They would prefer not to have to deal with these services, and none liked the idea of home banking via personal computer. It would be advisable for a senior program at the credit union to provide a "senior consultant" or "senior program service representative" to resolve questions related to the program on a one-on-one basis.

- Seniors typically have credit cards at financial institutions other than Acme Credit Union. They shop for the best interest rates and move their cards from institution to institution to get those rates. Consider offering and maintaining a lower interest rate on a credit card for members affiliated with an ACU senior program.

- If the program is instituted, ACU should consider other ways of increasing seniors' comfort levels in conducting business with the credit union. They do not like to wait in lines; perhaps a senior "express" line could be instituted. They are uncomfortable when conducting ATM transactions at night; consider improved lighting, and keep any shrubbery surrounding the ATM area trimmed to increase visibility as much as possible.

- Seminars related to retirement issues were considered important, but many stressed the need for better planning rather than trying to fit products to their financial situations *after* retirement. Preretirement financial seminars should be offered for members aged forty-five to fifty-five. Other seminar topics suggested by seniors included defensive driving, living wills, and Social Security issues.

- While only one of the two groups expressed interest in a seniors' newsletter associated with this program, it would be sensible to offer at least a quarterly publication to keep seniors abreast of additions to the program and what their available benefits are. These members are not frequently in the branches, and this would be a means of reaching them on a regular basis.

- Participants suggested several potential eligibility/pricing options. Two were suggested several times. One was basing free membership on having X number of services through the credit union (between three and five, for example). The second option would be maintaining a minimum balance across all Acme Credit Union deposit accounts in order to receive free membership. Suggested minimum balances ranged from $1,000 to $5,000. Anytime a member fell below the required number of services (option one) or the minimum deposit balance (option two), there would be a fee. Members were undecided on the amount of the service fee. These options should be viewed in terms of an analysis of senior members' existing services held, as well as their average deposit balances and overall profitability for the credit union. Such an analysis would provide better insight into which option would increase eligibility.

Executive Summary

Financial Institution Usage

Relationships with ACU

With few exceptions, members in both groups were long-term members of Acme Credit Union, typically having belonged for fifteen years or more. They also were similar in that they take advantage of a wide variety of the credit union's products and services. Only two advised that they have only savings accounts at ACU; the others have a number of ties to the credit union, including checking, RV loans, auto loans, credit cards, personal lines of credit, IRAs and/or CDs, as well as their savings accounts.

Affiliations with Other Institutions

Seniors are not, however, developing financial relationships solely with Acme Credit Union. Most acknowledged that they use other financial institutions as well for a variety of reasons, including convenience, rates, and longtime association with the institutions.

GROUP I

"First National Bank . . . I have a credit card . . . and a credit card with Bank of Anytown. . . . My checking accounts are at First National Bank. I mainly got savings and got started at Acme in my work because I discovered they can take it out of your check, which is . . . very nice. Money that you don't see, you don't use . . ."

"I have a checking account at Northwest Bank and a credit card through First Savings Bank. . . . I also have a credit card with Bank of Anytown, which I move around every six months to different banks—whoever is offering me the best interest rate."

"I have a checking and a savings account . . . mutual funds elsewhere."

"I have a credit card with First National Bank, and then I have a checking account there, too . . ."

"We have a checking account with First National Bank, and my husband also has savings and checking accounts through another credit union."

"Mutual funds and retirement funds and investments; credit cards through First Savings Bank and a trade association . . . credit consolidation loans that I got because of low interest rates out of state . . . out-of-state RV loan. . . . I came here twenty years ago and established an account with First Savings Bank, and I've always been real happy with what they've done . . ."

". . . At this time, I'm just at Acme Credit Union. I had been with First Savings Bank for credit cards, and I was at Commerce Bank for a long time before I went to Acme . . ."

GROUP II

"I use First Savings Bank . . . because it's close to where I live and it's more convenient . . ."

"First National Bank . . . we have IRAs at First National Bank, and I think we have one account left at Bank of Anytown."

"I have a safe-deposit box at First Savings Bank only because you don't have them here. . . . I would *like* to get everything all at one place."

"I have a mutual fund through a company called ABC. . . . They approached me through my school. Other than that, I don't deal with any other banks anymore. I did; I was with Bank of Anytown . . ."

Participants in the first group were a bit more conscious of loan and credit card rates, with several suggesting that they shop for rates, keeping an eye out for the best offer. For example, a woman has a credit card at 9.9 percent and moves it every six months to obtain the best rate. Another participant has an out-of-state consolidation loan and said this:

". . . I think I received something in the mail, and there had been several blurbs on TV about a year ago. They were doing some specials saying that if you shopped around, you could find some lower interest rates."

Primary Financial Institution

While senior members do use other financial institutions, when asked which one they would designate as their primary financial services provider, most named Acme Credit Union. Several others noted that their business is quite evenly split between the credit union and another institution, each being used for specific purposes (for example, direct deposit of checks, bill paying, checking versus savings, and convenience).

Among the other institutions cited as major providers for senior members were First National Bank, First Savings Bank, Bank of Anytown, and Northwest Bank.

Personal Contact with Staff

Focus group participants were asked how often they have personal contact (either by phone or in person) with staff at their primary institution(s). Although a few do so frequently, most were seldom in touch with staff personally, typically only two to three times per month. Some in the first group suggested that they feel that their institutions are actually *discouraging* personal contact:

GROUP I

"I don't [have personal contact] very often—just when I make withdrawals . . ."

"I go in a lot . . . probably at least once a week and sometimes twice a week."

"Most of our checks go in by direct deposit, so I don't have much contact, maybe once a month. . . . I think that First National Bank is encouraging you not to come in and confront the teller. They want you to use those machines, and I don't really like it; I'm not into 'modern age.'"

"When you're waiting in line, they come over and say, 'Can I show you how to use this? Wouldn't you like to use the ATM instead of waiting in line?' And they practically drag you over."

"Probably [I use] ATMs two to three, maybe four times per week with First Savings Bank . . . and personal contact, seems to me like a month or two months ago in the newspaper, First Savings Bank said they were going to start charging $2 per transaction with tellers, so I don't have a whole lot of transactions with tellers."

"Always [have personal contact] at the end of the week when I get paid."

GROUP II

"Very rarely do I have any personal contact with the people at the credit union; I would say once every six weeks *maybe*. But at the bank, probably two times per week."

Despite their generally limited personal contact with financial institutions' staffs, the members generally agreed that they *prefer* personal contact. Available time and the need for convenience may, however, force automated transactions. Some suggested that they would make the effort to have personal contact rather than use an ATM or bank by phone service.

GROUP I

"I like it [personal contact]; I prefer it."

"I get exasperated when you call up on the phone (I still think that's a personal contact) . . . and then you go through seventeen different menus because most times I don't have the time to put up with the inconvenience, quite honestly. . . . Sometimes, if I had a place to take my business, I'd be inclined to do that, because I think we've gotten so automated it's a hassle . . ."

"I think [personal contact] is very important for me anyway. At times when I cash my check I always am holding some money back, and I may want some change or this or that that the ATM machine doesn't provide me . . ."

"I prefer personal contact. I *never* use an ATM."

"I don't use the ATMs either. I want access to a real person when I want access, and I don't want to have to go through fifteen or twenty minutes of punching buttons; I resent that . . ."

"I like to go in and talk to the teller . . ."

"I like to . . . because when I'm talking to them, I can ask them [questions] . . ."

GROUP II

"It's important to me. I don't like machines . . ."

". . . I use the bank machine quite a bit . . . and I also call the automated phone banking system to find out what my balance is and what checks have come in and so forth, but it's not my *preferred* way. It's just that it's more convenient. . . . I like [personal contact]. . . . Whenever I go into the credit union, I find the tellers are very friendly and very helpful, and I really enjoy interaction with them much more than calling on the telephone system. It's just a matter of what's convenient, and since I don't live close to the credit union, I do what I can . . . the easiest way possible."

". . . I would prefer to have personal contact, just simply because I feel that it's a good idea for a person to get to know the people they do their banking with, but I think that's becoming a thing of the past . . . so I've given up, and now I use the phone system more than I ever did, and I use the ATM . . ."

"I personally like to talk to a teller, but at the same time, I use the phone system pretty regularly . . ."

"I like to talk to the person."

"I avoid contact with the credit union just because . . . I get sick and tired of punching those buttons. . . . That's why I go to the bank. I just take money from the credit union and put it in the bank. . . . I just despise . . . going through that menu . . . to talk to a human being. . . . I don't use an ATM."

". . . Picking up the phone and dialing the number is fine, because I hate to stand in line . . . but I like the contact . . ."

Attitudes Toward Automated Services

As their earlier comments indicated, many seniors will use automated financial services such as the ATM or telephone banking at least occasionally. These are not, however, preferred methods. None were interested at all in home banking via personal computers, and several cited concerns as well related to the use of ATMs and telephone banking services.

ATM COMMENTS

". . . I don't like [ATMs] in the first place because I think people can peek over and see what your number [is] . . ."

". . . One of the biggest security risks right now that you can do is an ATM . . ."

". . . Security is a big part of it."

"I'm always a little nervous about doing any banking at the ATM at night . . . there's something scary about that. You feel like you're sort of a 'sitting duck'. . ."

"I think the lighting is very important, and security is the reason that the only one I ever use is the one on Stuart Avenue that sits out in the middle of everything. . . . I won't go to any others."

TELEPHONE BANKING COMMENTS

". . . We tried to get in one night for a couple of hours because we really needed our money; it was there, but we couldn't get to it [at ACU], and we tried every number; we got the book out and went through the whole thing step by step and finally gave up in exasperation. And then, on Monday, we went over to our branch, and . . . they said, 'You weren't doing anything wrong. We were doing an audit; our computers were down.' And what I would say is that you'd better have a message that tells us that that is what is happening . . ."

"I like the phone service because I have my Social Security check deposited, and just to be sure it's in there, I sometimes call . . . to be certain before I enter it into my checkbook."

When asked what would increase their usage of automated services, participants cited improved lighting near ATMs. In addition, one member said that she would "like to see ATMs set up so if you had several accounts in different locations [institutions], if you could arrange to have the same PIN number . . ."

Lifestyle Issues

In each of the focus groups, only a few participants were already retired (four in Group I and three in Group II). Members were asked to describe some positive aspects of retirement, either current or anticipated. Freedom to do what they pleased was at the top of the list in both groups.

GROUP I

"I believe it's wonderful. . . . I get to do a lot of things that I couldn't do before. I volunteer, and I'm active in my church and make a lot of new friends. I think it's great! . . ."

"Travel; being able to go on the off-season . . . you can take off whenever you want to."

"I think it's positive in that you can have your time as your own; you don't have to get up and go to work each day . . ."

"I'm not retired, but my investments are making so much money for me that I know I'll be fine by the time I get there!"

GROUP II
In the second group, all of the participants generally agreed with one member who summed it up this way:

"The freedom of choice . . . is probably the most positive thing I can say about retirement."

On the negative side, health care and finances were seniors' primary concerns.

GROUP I

"You use . . . a lot of insurance. . . . You can't get dental insurance. . . . Eyes, ears, teeth . . . when you're working, it's covered."

"You'll probably have less income . . ."

"My income went down, but my expenses also went down."

GROUP II

"Health is important."

"If you didn't have some kind of an outlet, that could be very, very negative . . . some kind of a hobby or something."

"I think [lack of] contact with people."

In terms of retirement's effects on their financial needs, most discussed the need for better planning rather than a need for different products at retirement.

"My income went down temporarily, but I have tax-free annuities, which I got into in a big way, and as soon as I'm sixty, it'll go up. I'll be making *more*."

"I find it scary to look forward to because I don't think I'm going to have as much money to spend as I do now, and that's why I feel that I need to keep working, because I like to have money to keep doing things. . . . I am very concerned about how the financial end of it will work out once I retire . . ."

Several members also reiterated their concerns related to losing health insurance or not being able to cover that formidable expense:

". . . Your health insurance is a problem."

"I'm concerned about the health aspect of it . . ."

"[Re: health/medical bills] It's rather frightening. . . . I don't feel I'm very well prepared."

"Acme Credit Union should offer insurance."

General Attitudes Toward Senior Programs

Focus group participants were asked if they belonged to or were aware of any programs specifically targeted to seniors. In the first group, one mentioned a local hospital's senior program. Another also noted:

"I think First National Bank has put out some offers. . . . I threw them away. . . . It's for airline tickets, flying or traveling and staying in hotels across the country. . . . I don't know whether it's for seniors particularly or for anybody . . ."

One senior advised that her husband had a senior account at another credit union, and she didn't think that there were any charges associated with it. All participants in both groups expressed initial interest in Acme Credit Union offering a seniors' program.

Senior Program Features

Participants were asked, on an unaided basis, to identify products/ services to be included in the proposed program based on what they personally would need or use. Products/services not mentioned in the top-of-mind exercise were also considered. The table shows the proposed package features, based on the groups' discussions.

Desired Features of a Senior Program

(U) means unaided suggestion (no prompts were offered to members).

(A) means aided suggestion (members said it should be included after it was mentioned by the moderator).

Group I	Group II
(A) Free checking	(U) Free checking
(U) Free check printing	(U) Free check printing
(U) Share savings	(U) Share savings
(U) Free traveler's checks	(U) Free traveler's checks
(A) Free notary service	(A) Free notary service
(U) No-fee credit card	(U) No-fee credit card
(U) Debit card	(A) Debit card
(U) Free money orders	(U) Free money orders/cashier's checks
(U) ATM card	(A) ATM card [[U) free usage]
(A) Seminars	(U) Retirement planning seminars
(U) Health insurance	(A) Prescription/eyewear discounts
(U) Travel benefits (tours/discounts)	(U) Competitive interest on checking with minimum balance
(U) Financial adviser	(A) Safe-deposit box
(U) Low-rate loans	(U) Free funds transfers
(A) Senior newsletter	
(U) No annual fee for seniors' program/package	

Both groups expressed similar expectations for an Acme Credit Union senior program, with an emphasis on low-cost or free benefits. The first group, while interested in health insurance through the credit union, recognized that this might not be feasible and that they would expect a payment to be associated with that particular benefit.

Seminar suggestions covered a variety of topics, including Social Security, living wills, defensive driving, and retirement planning.

The second group was not overly interested in a newsletter. In contrast, the first group generally agreed with a member who said, "If you're going to offer all of this, I guess [we] should get a newsletter."

Eligibility and Pricing

Members were asked what they would consider to be fair eligibility requirements or program costs based on a program with the benefits they were personally interested in.

GROUP I

"A minimum balance in a combination of accounts."

"First National Bank has a thousand-dollar minimum balance; if you drop below that, you pay a fee."

". . . I think that's all right [$1,000]. And that medical thing, I don't expect that it would be free . . . *availability* would be membership based."

"You might have a different combination of benefits depending upon a different scale of how much you had."

When asked about a fee for the program if they fell below the minimum balance, Group I's responses varied:

"$30 a year."

"I think it would be very difficult to have this fee vary every month . . ."

"Maybe they could consider how many of the different . . . things you're taking part in. If you have an auto loan and a credit card and you have your checking and savings . . . say you had at least five, there'd be no service fee."

GROUP II

"If you have three or four different services . . ."

". . . At least meet what the competition's doing."

"In order to receive the services, you'd have to have your Social Security or your retirement check deposited. . . . that would be a 'must' to get the services."

Most in Group II felt that $5,000 would be a fair minimum balance based on combined deposit accounts.

Assuming the pricing options discussed and the benefits they preferred, all participants in both groups indicated that they would be likely to join an Acme Credit Union senior program. Most also agreed that they would consolidate accounts from other institutions to join such a program.

Member Suggestions

Senior members were asked to identify the one thing that would make their own relationship with ACU stronger. While several offered suggestions, many also noted that they were satisfied with their credit union relationships as they currently exist.

GROUP I

"More branches . . . near me! . . ."

"The insurance would be a big pull . . ."

". . . with First National Bank, I get my checks every month."

"Probably a no-fee, low-interest credit card."

"I don't like having everything in the same place."

"Lower interest rates on loans over a certain amount."

"How about higher interest rates on deposits?"

GROUP II

"The only thing I can think of is a safe-deposit box . . ."

". . . overdraft [protection] on debit card."

"I'm satisfied with the services."

"I don't know of anything off-hand."

"There isn't anything I could say I'd change. I'm very comfortable with it . . ."

A member in Group II also suggested that Acme Credit Union should make its checking account services competitive with those of private banks.

Communications

FOCUS GROUP STUDY

Executive Summary Report

Contents

Introduction
Background

Methodology

Key Findings

Executive Summary
General Familiarity with Cell Phones and Airtime Offers

Pager Usage

Perceived Benefits of Cellular Phones

Benefits Testing

Airtime Provider Awareness and Perceived Image

Media Profile

General Opinions About Phone Ads

Ad Concept Testing

Program Evaluation

Introduction

Background

Focus Inc. was commissioned by ABCellular to conduct focus groups to test its pricing and advertising concepts among men in the Anytown market. The purpose of the research is to evaluate the target market's awareness of cellular options and to identify the best means of reaching men who typically do not use a cellular phone.

The study included these specific objectives:

- Determining general familiarity with cellular phones and program offerings

- Evaluating pager usage in the market

- Identifying perceived benefits of cellular phones

- Testing benefits associated with the proposed program

- Evaluating awareness and perceived image of airtime providers

- Determining the target market's media habits (television, radio, and print)

- Discussing recall and general opinions related to phone advertisements (long distance, cellular, etc.)

- Testing radio and print advertising concepts

- Evaluating interest levels regarding ABCellular's program

Methodology

Two focus groups were conducted in Anytown on May 27. All participants were males and were randomly recruited from the Anytown area. They were screened to meet requirements identified by the client as fitting their target market: falling between the ages of eighteen and thirty-nine with average annual incomes before taxes between $25,000 and $40,000. They also could not personally own a cellular telephone. In addition, participants were screened to confirm that neither they nor anyone in their households were employed by a cellular communications or advertising firm and none had attended a focus group discussion within the past six months.

Recruiting was conducted by telephone utilizing the professional interviewing services of Focus Inc. Fourteen participants were recruited for each group, ten participated in each. Groups were conducted at Focus Inc.'s facility in Anytown. Each group lasted approximately ninety minutes and was audio- and videotaped for reporting purposes. Each participant received a co-op payment of $45.

Key Findings

- Males in the Anytown market view cellular phones as a luxury item rather than as a necessity. They are perceived as high-cost items, particularly in terms of airtime bills. Pagers are generally considered a more cost-effective alternative.

- In some cases, cellular phones are considered to be a supplement to pager usage rather than a replacement for them. Given this perception, the first advertisement comparing phones to pagers is likely to be less effective in this market.

Participants preferred the second ad and saw it as offering far more information specifically about cellular phones.

- Participants would use cellular phones primarily for business purposes or emergencies. Advertising that emphasizes the convenience of a cellular phone for such situations would be most effective in this target market.

- Lower-cost airtime was considered to be the most important benefit offered by ABCellular.

- Other issues that participants felt should be covered in the advertising were the quality and type of phone offered, the quality of service and airtime, and the warranty and service available for the phone itself.

- The reputation of a cellular airtime provider is extremely important in this market. Participants said they want to use a company they have heard of, and many felt that company size was related to reputation.

- Participants were not heavy television viewers, but most listen frequently to the radio, particularly to "oldies" or alternative music programming. In terms of newspapers, most read the *Anytown Crier*, but the *City Observer* was also mentioned occasionally.

- This market does pay attention to advertising, but it is primarily price that catches their attention in any media format. Pictures of phones are a plus, however, as they attract their attention and give an idea of what is being offered. Participants claimed that they will shop around for the "best deal," but despite claiming to understand the deposit/contract process involved with cellular telephone programs, they seem hooked on the idea of getting a "free phone."

- Given the program information and various options presented, most participants believed that they would take a closer look at what ABCellular offers. Price will, however, continue to be the deciding factor in their final decisions regarding cellular phone and airtime purchases.

Executive Summary

General Familiarity with Cellular Phones and Airtime Offers

While none of the participants personally owned a cellular phone, one advised that he uses a cellular phone for work. He was, however, unable to identify the airtime provider, as he does not personally pay the monthly bill. Many of the men had previously considered getting a cellular phone for a variety of reasons and then decided not to do so:

"Business . . . for me."

"It's convenient, too."

". . . The deal was so good that I was going to do it, but I said, 'I don't really need one . . . '"

"A lot of it has to do with being married, too . . . [your wife] can find you anywhere."

"Convenient . . . you don't have to stop and use a pay phone."

"I thought about it, but the airtime can get really expensive, so I just got a pager instead."

Pager Usage

Several of the participants currently have pagers, while one had had one in the past. They all used them primarily for personal purposes, although one also used it for business. The participant who no longer had the pager explained why this was the case:

"When I got it, it was for business, but . . . it ended up being personal. That's why I got rid of it."

When asked how they selected their particular pagers, they typically indicated that a special deal or advertisement caught their attention. In one case, the participant received his pager through his company.

"I needed something because I'm never at home . . . so I decided to get a pager. The company I went to had a good deal going on, and I got it."

"Mine was advertised also . . ."

Participants selected pagers over cellular phones mainly because they perceived pagers to cost far less.

"Cost . . . because cellular phones are . . . more expensive, not to mention the airtime can get really expensive, especially if you talk a lot."

"Same—[cell phones are] too expensive."

Most participants' friends have pagers, but in many instances they also have cellular phones. Participants were asked if they felt that cellular phones were considered more of a status symbol than pagers:

"Sure it is. . . . It's gotten to the point now, if you have a pager . . . it's normal now. Now if you've got a phone, they take a second look . . ."

"Yeah, because it's more costly."

"It's just a sign of being cool."

Perceived Benefits of Cellular Phones

When asked what they would use a cellular phone for if they had one, most believed that they would use it primarily for business purposes or emergency situations:

"Mine would be business."

"Business."

"Personal calls."

"Business, but also emergencies."

"Emergencies, that's about it."

"Personal, business—either way."

"I think more business and more for convenience; like if I really have to use a phone, then I'd use the cell phone."

Participants with pagers said they might keep their pagers even if they did get a cellular phone.

"I think so . . . I'm not sure . . . I've never known of call waiting or anything as far as that on a cellular phone, and I know you'll never get a busy signal on a pager . . ."

"No, I wouldn't [keep the pager] because of the high cellular phone bill."

"I probably would . . . I have voice mail. . . . If they leave a message, I can call and see what it is, and that only takes a matter of a few seconds."

Benefits Testing

Participants were read a list of potential program benefits and asked to rate each one on a scale of 1 to 3, with 1 being "not at all important" to them and 3 being "very important." Average ratings are presented in the table. It is important to remember that these groups do not represent a statistical sampling, so these results are not actually quantitative.

Ratings of Potential Program Benefits

Benefit	Average Rating
Lower-cost airtime	3.0
Free cellular phone	2.7
Lower deposit	2.6
Shorter contract period	1.1

Most participants agreed that they would reconsider getting a cellular phone if they found a program offering these benefits. However, price remained the prevailing concern:

"I'd sign up real quick, if those were the options offered, sure."

". . . I'd still have to see what the price was."

"That's it! The price is the bottom line."

They also suggested a number of characteristics they felt would be important to cover in a program of this type:

"What type of phone they're offering."

"Quality of the phone."

"Quality of the service and airtime."

"What's the guarantee on the phone? . . . like if I broke it or lost it, or how they would cover it . . . and the durability of the phone."

"The service."

"Do you own . . . the phone?"

". . . The quality of the airtime; how far the airtime [reaches] . . . what's the distance of the airtime? . . ."

Most agreed that coverage was important:

"You don't want to be stranded out there and have no access."

Airtime Provider Awareness and Perceived Image

Participants believe that the reputation of a cellular airtime provider would be extremely important when making their cellular choice:

"It would be *very* important."

"They would have to be reputable."

"I would rather go with somebody I've heard of."

Likewise, there was a general consensus that they would shop for air-time rather than take the first offer they came across.

While participants felt that company size was related to reputation and that they would be more familiar with larger companies, one man had this suggestion:

"The problem is the bigger the company is, usually the higher your costs are."

Media Profile

Focus group participants were not heavy television viewers, with most watching only a few specific shows ranging from sitcoms to news and sports events. They listen to radio programming more frequently, with participants' tastes ranging from "oldies" to alternative music. Few mentioned the same station twice, but four of the participants listen to the radio all day, while others stated that they listen regularly during their drives to and from work.

The *Anytown Crier* is the most frequently read newspaper. A few participants also read the *City Observer*.

General Opinions About Phone Ads

Participants were asked to list any advertising they have seen or heard related to telephones, long distance, cellular airtime, etc. Their responses were weighted heavily toward long distance and collect calling advertisements. One person also noted that he gets a lot of long-distance service offers over the phone such as "We'll give you $50 to sign up for our long-distance service."

In general, participants felt that they are usually able to determine what these advertisements are selling:

"They put [in] pictures, usually of the phone or whatever."

"On the radio, they'll tell you."

One man felt that it was more difficult than that, however:

"You've got to be a really sharp listener . . ."

because the advertisements don't always list all of the details from the "fine print."

When asked what catches their eye in telephone/cellular service advertising, nearly all of the focus group participants cited price.

". . . How much you've got to pay . . ."

"The price."

"The monthly bill."

"Probably the price."

"The picture . . . if I see a phone . . ."

"The price, yeah, but I think only if I was in the market for a cellular phone would I actually look at the ad."

"The phone and the price."

"The price and the picture."

There was also general agreement that having a phone pictured in an advertisement was a positive aspect "because you might have this great price and this great offer, and you have a lousy phone."

Ad Concept Testing

Price again played a major role in determining where participants would go if they were shopping for a cellular telephone:

"The cheapest place."

"Where the lowest price is."

"Just shop around, try to get a better deal."

"The cheapest option . . ."

"Look around, I guess."

Participants claimed to be aware of the deposit and contract process typically associated with cellular telephone sales.

". . . It's like the old cliché, you don't get something . . . for nothing. . . . That's what turns me off. It says 'free this,' 'free that.' Forget it! . . . I'll pass it up."

Still, later conversations seemed to indicate that participants are not as familiar with these procedures as they felt they were.

Many stated that they would choose to buy their own phone or get one for free and then shop around for their airtime rates.

In terms of the print advertising, the second advertisement presented was the preferred concept, mainly because it provided more information specifically about cellular phones.

"This one catches my eye right off the bat because . . . more writing . . ."

"It gives you a lot more information."

"It would catch your eye."

"More informative."

"This one is done real well."

All generally agreed that they would at least call in for more details, having seen this particular advertisement.

Program Evaluation

Several ABCellular program options were introduced to members, along with the cost variations that depended on the different cellular phones styles available. While participants seemed somewhat surprised at what was initially perceived as high pricing, upon further discussion, most believed that they would give the program a second look. Price-related concerns remained, however, with a few participants suggesting that they would simply go elsewhere to buy their phone and then shop for airtime. This further indicates their confusion regarding the purchase process for cellular phones and airtime.

> ". . . I can go buy a phone at an electronics store for $49 and then get my own airtime . . ."

> "But a lot of these places are offering you *free* phones."

Ultimately, participants were asked, based on all of the information they had covered during the group, if their interest level in a cellular phone had changed since the start of the session. Their interest was piqued, although not strongly, and price remained the crucial factor for many participants:

> "The price is all right. I'd really have to consider it if I was in the market, it's hard to say; but it's a good deal . . . I would consider it."

> "I would probably consider it . . ."

> "What about service, parts, and repairs?"

> "The prices on the phones are a little bit high, but it'd be a good deal."

> "I'd probably shop for my own phone and look around and see what the competition has . . ."

> ". . . I'd shop for my own phone."

"I wouldn't buy one."

"To me, at that price, I'm just paying for the phone and nothing else coming with it."

"I would really look into this, but I'd have some other questions like is it limited airtime? How long do I have? . . . I would have to look into it more thoroughly."

Software Focus Group

Executive Summary Report

Contents

Introduction

Background Information

ABC Research was commissioned by Software Design Inc. (SDI) to conduct and evaluate the results of two focus groups. The overall purpose of the research study was to obtain user input regarding SDI's new workstation software product prior to its scheduled release. Specific objectives included the following:

- Identification of potential users' needs (unaided)

- Evaluation of potential users' responses to the look and feel of the sample screens

- Discussion regarding potential users' perceptions of the product's possible effects on their productivity

- Solicitation of potential users' suggestions for product improvements and/or modifications

Methodology

Two focus groups were held with persons who work in customer service, collections, and telemarketing positions that require them to devote 50 percent or more of their time to using a computer to obtain related records. One group consisted of employees at firms that are currently Software Design Inc. customers. The second group was drawn from a list of firms identified as non-SDI customers currently utilizing competitive systems.

Ten recruits attended the 6:00 P.M. group on September 25 in Anytown, while eight participated in the 8:00 P.M. group on the same date. All participants were compensated $50 for their time and input. Both focus groups were audio- and videotaped for reporting purposes.

It is important to bear in mind throughout this report that the participants are potential users of the type of product being evaluated. They are not, however, in decision-making or influencing positions and would not determine the purchase of this product. Their comments should be considered only in the context of providing input to make the product more user-friendly.

In addition, it is important when reviewing focus group analyses to remember that the information compiled from such group discussions is *not quantifiable*. In other words, comparisons should not be made within groups comparing individuals' comments (e.g., in this instance, telemarketers versus collection agents). The intent of this particular study is basically to determine whether the proposed product is adequately user-friendly or modifications should be considered. Comparisons, where applicable, are made between users employed by SDI customers and users employed by firms currently using competing systems.

Recommendations

- Group participants were extremely concerned with the speed and efficiency of the new system. In many cases, they are dissatisfied with these aspects of their current systems and would be receptive to a new system if it would increase their productivity. They saw many features in the new product that met this need, but there is a great degree of discomfort with using a mouse versus pressing keys. They generally felt that the mouse would slow them down, as they are used to pressing a specific key to get to where they need to go. It is important that the system provide users with an option to type in commands and comments, along with the option of using the mouse.

- The Help feature on the new system is not generally viewed as necessary. Tailor the Help messages to the novice user, keeping the instructions basic and simple to follow. Experienced users would not be likely to utilize this resource very often, if at all.

- Participants expressed a great deal of concern regarding the proposed system's callback capabilities. Users emphasized the need to be able to set callbacks for themselves, ensuring that a scheduled callback would come back to their own line. This was particularly important to telemarketing representatives, who stand to earn commissions from successful sales calls. But although this theme recurs among the users in both groups, it is not necessarily a good idea to include this capability. From a management standpoint, this is not necessarily as productive, as calls may be delayed or missed entirely due to staff changes, representatives on vacation, heavy call volumes, and so forth. Despite user preferences, it would be best to consider this option only after determining management preferences regarding this subject.

- The option to send facsimiles and letters is viewed as "nice," but in reality it is not likely to be utilized frequently. Users feel that their supervisors would be reluctant to allow them the authority to send information to customers/contacts without prior approval and review of the content. It is a good feature to have available, but not necessarily a strong marketing point.

- Participants frequently mentioned the need for extensive message fields. The moderator had to continually remind them that the screens are tailored to meet the requirements of each individual firm. This point should, however, be dealt with when working on developing firms' individual systems. Recommend more space for messages and notes to promote better record keeping.

- Include editing capabilities such as a spell-checker, thesaurus, and "insert" feature. Users felt that they would use these features regularly and wanted to have them available to edit their comments.

- Many participants were interested in E-mail capabilities. While they do not view this as a necessity, it could increase users' efficiency by allowing them to send messages to other representatives and supervisors rather than leaving their stations to talk.

- Users were concerned about including productivity-reporting capabilities. Many currently have this capability on their systems, while others have to determine their productivity themselves following each shift. SDI's system should provide a means of calculating and reporting such information as calls per hour and sales per hour.

Detailed Findings

Current Systems and Software

Participant Profiles

Participants represented a variety of positions related to both inbound and outbound calling: telemarketing/sales, collections, and customer/technical service. The initial group comprised SDI customers. Several participants in this group are utilizing a program that in many instances sounded similar to the product being tested. Two other participants, both collection agents, mentioned similar capabilities and stated that they will soon be adding a new system that will allow them to "request all available information at the PC."

Customer group participants handle inbound calls in terms of service calls, account updates, credit/account queries, and basic customer service issues. On the outbound side, collection agents initiate calls pertaining to overdue accounts ranging in age from ninety days to over two years or more. Other outbound activities include telemarketing, surveys and opinion polls, and lead generation.

Noncustomer participants are handling similar calls, with inbound calls relating to customer service and requests for referrals. In terms of outbound calls, these representatives are handling calls related to telemarketing, lead generation, and collections.

In both cases, customer and noncustomer, most representatives are full-time employees, putting in thirty to forty hours per week on their respective systems. Both groups generally agreed that it took them only a few days to two weeks to initially learn their systems, although many were also quick to add that *mastering* their systems is an ongoing process. There were a few exceptions to the brief learning curves, where representatives advised that it took them two or three months to learn their systems and then at least one year to master them.

Handling Objections

The customer group briefly discussed how representatives making outbound sales calls handle objections on their current systems:

"When we use our system, we have a script. . . . They can put the entire script on the screen, but very seldom will they bother to put in possible objections as well . . ."

". . . and at our company we can do that . . . with the new access that we have. . . . I can punch a key [to deal with different situations]."

"We have a screen that we can bring up that will have objections . . ."

"We have nothing on the monitor; we have a book . . ."

To allow for a more in-depth review of the new system, this issue was not covered in the noncustomer group.

Likes and Dislikes About Current Systems

Prior to viewing the new product demo, group participants were asked to identify the positive and negative features of their current systems. Customers' notable comments included the following:

LIKES

"We have access to many systems at one location."

"The fact that it dials all the time, and it goes through, and until it finds a live body . . . it doesn't give you the call . . ."

"Rich database."

"Really fast."

"Very efficient."

DISLIKES

"We have to do a lot of entries that are actual typing."

"Limitation of data available and limitation of data that you can add. . . . Case in point: . . . we're doing one survey, and those guys kept saying, 'We're all network users,' . . . and a month and a half later the manager says, '. . . We've got to get a database on network users, but we can't find one.' Well, we had just built one . . . if we could have kept it . . ."

". . . You're basically chained to a desk."

"Remembering too many screens."

"Lack of control."

Other comments related to their systems being too slow, and one participant mentioned wanting to be able to stand up to type during the calls.

In the customer group, participants were also asked what could be changed to make their systems easier to use. In several cases, their companies had already initiated such changes. Others are anticipating changes to their systems within the next year.

Noncustomer participants offered similar comments in terms of their likes and dislikes about their current systems:

LIKES

"Ours is really easy; if you don't know a lot about computers, you can still fill out the screen . . . user-friendly."

"Ours never goes down."

"Easy to access."

"Reliable."

"Convenient order entry setup."

"With ours, on consumer accounts we can enter pages and pages of notes."

DISLIKES

". . . We should have more information on our screens. . . . I think the info's in there. I'm not sure whether it's just that the software can't pull it up. . . . I don't know . . ."

"There are codes that we don't have in the computer, so we have to post them somewhere and look to find them. . . . that slows the calls down . . ."

". . . It's difficult to make comments while you're on the phone. . . . The way our system is set up, you don't have to terminate the call to make comments, but you have to do several things, and while you're trying to carry on a conversation with somebody . . . I end up just using a piece of paper . . ."

"Not enough product information."

New Product Evaluation

Participants in both focus group sessions viewed a demonstration of the current as well as the potentially available features of the SDI product. In the customer group, participants were advised that the second segment of the demo consisted of future possibilities rather than currently available features. In the noncustomer group, to eliminate confusion, the demonstration was treated as one demo of features without identifying those that have not yet been incorporated into the program.

This summary will consolidate similar topics for ease of analysis.

Accessing Information

Group members currently access information in a few different ways.

"[Typing] four letters to get the screen you want."

"You can pull it up. If [a customer has] a question about a product . . . you can mouse onto the product, and you can pull it up and talk about any feature of that product . . ."

Several noncustomer group participants mentioned using macros to access customer data:

"I like our macros . . . it takes you right there . . ."

Mouse Usage

The customer group would welcome the mouse being used with the system. One company currently uses a mouse with its program, and the others generally agreed that this would be a positive feature to include:

"We'd prefer having a mouse."

"Definitely."

Most participants in the second group (noncustomers) were less receptive to this technology, as few were currently using a mouse in any aspect of their jobs and they are comfortable with their current methods:

"We have macros that are like '10,' '8,' '7,' . . . saves a lot of time."

". . . Once I know where a product is in the list . . . the macro . . . the 'shift-F10' or whatever . . . rather than scrolling down through the whole thing each time, I'm able to save a heck of a lot of time . . ."

"You do tend to start having just automatic responses to situations, and that's one of the things that gets tiresome in a lot of programs is having to always pull down something or having to always . . . highlight something in order to type over it . . ."

"You wear such 'grooves' in your mind, your fingers just do what they need to do to get where you're going . . ."

"[The mouse is] too slow."

"If you're in a routine task that you have learned . . . then going to the mouse all the time is going to slow you down a lot . . ."

"I'm just really clumsy with a mouse. . . . I can type so much quicker."

"We have function keys, and the function keys are very efficient."

As the conversation continued, however, the noncustomers also identified instances where having a mouse would be useful, as in this example:

"On the flip side, if I want a screen . . . rather than tabbing a million times to get where I want to go, I would reach for the mouse . . ."

They acknowledged that "different people use computers differently" and ultimately agreed that the program should allow for both typing commands and the use of the mouse:

". . . If you allow for us to do it either way, we'll be happy!"

Help Capabilities

Reactions to the Help capabilities offered by the new system were mixed. The general consensus in both groups was that it is a good feature for the novice but not really necessary or useful if you have been on the job for some time:

"We have it, and I never use it."

". . . [Perhaps have] a novice and an expert mode."

". . . If you're new, maybe you'd use it a little more, but if you're already there, if you know all the scripts pretty much, then it's not as useful . . ."

Some telemarketing representatives, on the other hand, felt that, given their constant flow of temporary staff, Help might be more valuable:

"The Help capability for us would be fantastic."

Customer group participants also discussed customizing Help for themselves, as this would assist them with selecting the correct form letters for specific cases.

Specific Features

Features that drew the most comments were the keypad, scheduling of callbacks, the calendar, and fax/letter capabilities.

Keypad

Currently neither customers nor noncustomers have the capability to circumvent voice-mail systems reached during outbound calls using their systems. When asked how they deal with this problem, they all gave similar responses:

". . . You have to get out of the call."

"We have a program where you can't, at least according to *our* people. . . . There was for a while a fluke way it was working on a couple of calls, but I couldn't get it to be consistent . . ."

"You just call them back . . ."

"We just disconnect."

"It hangs up, and we have to call them back."

Callbacks

Scheduling callbacks was an important issue for attendees in both groups. Some participants noted that their systems allowed scheduling of callbacks in a limited manner:

"If somebody says, 'Call me back in ten minutes,' our system doesn't allow that."

". . . If you can actually 'status' it to call them back, it'll call them back during the next shift."

They generally appeared to like the proposed system's callback feature:

"I like the idea of putting in a specific callback time."
However, some concerns were voiced:

"What happens if you're on a call within that sixty-minute period [when the callback is scheduled], then this call starts to go through?"

"I don't want to set up a call that's going to give me big bucks and then have somebody else get the call; I did all the groundwork."

"On your calendar, when you schedule a callback in there, if you could have it come back to the person that scheduled that call in the first place . . . it gives you a leg up because you've already talked to the person, and you know that they're expecting to have someone talk to them again. It'd be great if it could do it . . ."

Calendar
Participants generally liked the calendar feature as demonstrated in their groups:

". . . What I liked probably most was the calendar . . ."

"I like the calendar because that way I can say, 'Well, you called us yesterday and asked the same question . . .'"

"I love that calendar."

Fax/Letter Capabilities

Of participants in both groups, only a few advised that they have facsimile capabilities from their PCs, and it was not clear whether this was actually a feature of their current system. None of the others have this capability, although some have the ability to generate letters using their current systems. Faxing was generally viewed as a positive addition:

> "Nice option because I've had customers say, 'Can you send me a fax?'"

> "That would be a nice option."

Alternately, a few participants felt it was an unnecessary luxury, as they would not be allowed to use it:

> ". . . My supervisor would never let me send a fax straight through . . ."

> "Our managers would be very nervous . . ."

Product Suggestions

Focus group participants discussed several additional features that many viewed as important for inclusion in the new system: editing, E-mail, security log-on, and productivity statistics.

Editing

Users would like editing capabilities for their entries, including a spell-checker, thesaurus, and an "insert" feature. They also want a way to mark their files with their initials:

". . . If when we logged on, anything we touched would automatically stick our name on it."

"I like the idea of being able to mark a file . . ."

E-Mail
Customer group users discussed E-mail capabilities, noting that this would be helpful:

"Does this system . . . allow you to send the information on the computer . . . ?"

"Do you have something called 'E-mail,' where you can E-mail each other?"

Security Log-On
The product demo did not cover security log-on in detail, so when one noncustomer group participant noted, "I don't see any security log-on procedure," others in that group jumped in and stressed that system security has to be a crucial aspect of any system for them.

Productivity Statistics
Participants from the noncustomer group identified productivity reporting as an essential feature for their firms. Since many users currently have this available with their systems, it is considered a valuable feature:

"Our phones do that for us . . ."

". . . At the end of a shift . . . you can have all that information in front of you . . . all the different call results, how many of each one, how long on each call . . ."

Given the importance of this information to them, they asked about how the new system would propose to handle this issue:

"Another thing I haven't seen is the whole area of productivity statistics, such as calls per hour, sales per hour, and so on."

"It'd be really nice for us, because we have to figure out our productivity ourselves by hand and it would really help."

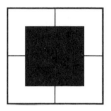

Index

The American Marketing Association is the world's largest and most comprehensive professional association of marketers. With over 45,000 members, the AMA has more than 500 chapters throughout North America. The AMA sponsors 25 major conferences per year, covering topic ranging from the latest trends in customer satisfaction measurement to business-to-business and service marketing, attitude research and sales promotion, and publishes nine major marketing publications.

For further information on the American Marketing Association, call TOLL FREE at 1-800-AMA-1150.

Or write to:
American Marketing Association
311 S. Wacker Drive, Suite 5800
Chicago, Illinois 60606-2266
(800) 262-1150
(800) 950-0872 FAX